THE ART

of

GIVING UP

An Unconventional
Spiritual Discipline

THE ART
of
GIVING UP

An Unconventional
Spiritual Discipline

Kai Eilert

THE ART
—— *of* ——
GIVING UP
**AN UNCONVENTIONAL
SPIRITUAL DISCIPLINE**

Dedication

This book is dedicated to my wife and children.

To my wife: Next to Jesus, you have been one of the greatest examples of giving up I've had the privilege of learning from. It's an honor to live a life of sacrifice with you.

To my children: My hope is that you would follow me as I learn to follow Christ. May the blessings of giving up in Jesus' name follow you all the days of your life.

Contents

Acknowledgments

Thank you, my King Jesus, for giving up everything so I can gain all that God desires for me.

Thank you, my church family (Central City Assembly), for allowing me to test the material in this book on you first in sermon form.

Thank you, Dad and Mom, for being my first model of giving up for the sake of others. Without your sacrifice as exceptional parents I wouldn't be the husband, father, or pastor I am today.

Introduction

I'm not sure the hour, but early one morning before the sun started to peak over the mountain sky, I woke up to the startling thought that I needed to give up in my marriage. What's more startling is that I believed that it was God who gave me this thought. For whatever reason God likes to deposit profound thoughts and ideas in my mind when I'm not fully awake.

All day after the thought entered my mind, I couldn't stop thinking about it. Give up in my marriage? What kind of marriage advice is that, God? But the more I thought about it, the more I realized how true it is. The more we give up and sacrifice in our marriages, in our parenting, in our careers, the more we gain of God. Jesus gave up everything for the sake of the world and look how glorious his giving up turned out for him and for humanity.

I realized that God was revealing to me a foundational truth that is central to Christ's life but also Christian living. A spiritual discipline if you will. I also realized I had never read a book or heard a sermon, let alone a series of sermons all on the topic of giving up. Again, this was startling because if Jesus lived a life of total surrender and if Jesus is our perfect model for how we should live today, then why hadn't I heard more about it.

It felt like this thought of giving up quickly turned into a mandate from God to speak on a topic that the greater Church needed to hear and learn from. And thus The Art of Giving Up was born. What started out as an idea, turned into a series of sermons, and now has turned into the book you hold in your hands now.

My prayer for you as you read this book is that you would be moved like I was, from feeling startled to understanding your need for surrender. And as you grow in mastering the art of giving up you'll experience the blessed life that God has for you in a life of surrender.

Much Love and Many Blessings,

Kai

RAISE YOUR FLAG

This might sound like a silly question, but do you enjoy giving up? Do you just love throwing in the towel? I must admit that there is only one area in my life where I actually enjoy calling it a day: running. I might have the body type of a runner, but my spirit is in open rebellion. I *loathe* running. Still, I was required to do a lot of it while in the Air Force. We did some serious training, and parts of it were bearable. Make me do pushups, sit-ups, pull-ups, or planks. Fine! But running? Just don't.

Despite my aversion to sprinting and racing, one of my greatest achievements in the Air Force happened while I was running. I was required to complete a 5K. I was proud of it partly because I finished it in about twenty-three minutes, which averages out to less than five minutes per mile. I was also thrilled to finish second only to this guy who was built like an Olympian.

What really made it feel like an achievement, however, is that I had walked about a third of the distance and still got a great time.

When I run, it's definitely a mind-over-matter scenario. My mind tells me that running doesn't really matter, and I respond, "You know what, mind? You're right! You win!" I am totally okay with giving up. I feel so much better when I stop running. I have holy peace of mind. When it comes to running, I have undoubtedly mastered the art of giving up.

We all have things we don't mind giving up on. Maybe you have a deep sense of tranquility about relinquishing vegetables, extra paperwork, or your old car. When it comes to things that matter, though, I don't think anyone truly likes giving up. We don't take great pride in quitting our jobs or forgetting about our weight-loss goals, which is because we live in a society that places high value on perseverance. The ability to "keep on keepin' on" often leads to success in the categories the world values.

Think about all the fireworks that your neighbors launch into the sky on Independence Day. We wouldn't be celebrating if our Founding Fathers had given up. A glance at US history shows you that they had plenty of opportunities to surrender. The thirteen colonies were outmatched by Great Britain in all the critical arenas: resources, manpower, strategy, and training. It's miraculous that we won and remain a country to this day. Because of our forefathers' vision, bravery, and unwillingness to give up, the US became independent. Even in modern times, a flag fluttering in the breeze lets us know that we don't answer to any other nation.

Everywhere you look in the world, the gospel of perseverance is preached. We are told that the worst thing you can do in life is give up. We are coached that we can do anything we put our minds to. We must keep going. We can't let go. The best people hustle and grind until their dreams come true. Persistence is viewed as the highest of virtues. By contrast, giving up is seen as a sign of weakness, a transparent excuse to be lazy. The progress that matters doesn't happen if you stop trying. It won't result in anything but lack.

I think we can all agree on the value of persistence when it comes to our professional and personal endeavors. Yet there are some drawbacks to the kind of perseverance that the world preaches. This brand of unrelenting effort has led to heightened stress, increased fatigue, and mental and physical illness. It has resulted in the dismantling of relationships and the absence of parents. Many believe that if they take a break from work, they are going to fall behind on their tasks. Someone else is going to get ahead of them in the rat race, and their goals will never be reached.

Is that kind of perseverance compatible with the Gospel of the Kingdom of God, though? Does our heavenly Father value determination over surrender? Which of these two will lead to the success and blessing you're hoping to look back on when the sun sets, and you're sitting in your rocking chair at the end of your life?

I believe that God absolutely values persistence. I think blessing and success in the Kingdom of God do come as a result of hard work. Yet what we see time and again in scripture is that perseverance itself is never enough. There is, in fact, an art and a reward when we surrender, but it's not the kind of surrender you might think it is.

Start with Self-Surrender

In today's world, the phrase "deny yourself" doesn't bring up delightful feelings. Thoughts of staring at a commercial for new workout gear while I throw on old sweats come to mind. So does walking past that new car lot to purchase a family-friendly clunker. It might also bring up images of stuffing yourself into a button-down shirt and trudging off to work in the morning instead of lounging in your fleecy pajamas. Self-denial doesn't sound like fun, but we understand it as necessary.

Sometimes, God does ask us to give up certain pleasures for His sake. Fasting is a form of that which I believe is an important part of walking with Jesus and growing in our faith. We give up food for a period to focus on prayer and reading the Word. We allow ourselves to feel hungry because we want to gain humility and spiritual strength, but fasting is more like stuff-surrender, and not self-surrender.

Self-surrender, in the context of our faith, is a total relinquishing of our own will to that of God the Father. It is turning from our own visions and leaning on the will of God. The Bible tells us to "[5] Trust in the Lord with all your heart, and do not lean on your own understanding. [6] In all your ways acknowledge him, and he will make straight your paths" (Proverbs 3:5-6). This is a wonderful promise! If we are willing to let go of our own "making sense" of things and of our manufactured answers to our problems, God will make our paths straight. He will provide answers. He will rescue you in a way you never dreamed of because that is the mysterious way He works.

Self-surrender is a total relinquishing of our own will to that of God the Father.

When children are small, they follow their parents to church or eat what is prepared for dinner. They are helpless without mature adults who can provide them with what is best for their well-being. Left to their own devices, they would likely choose to fill their little tummies with candy and their impressionable minds with vapid TV shows. Similarly, before sin entered the world, self-surrender was the default of humanity. Human beings were dependent upon the wisdom of their all-knowing heavenly Father, surrendering their less-perfect will to His. There was an implicit trust in His love and provision. We obeyed His laws, and the result was a harmonious universe where work was meaningful, rest was expected, and God Himself walked with His people in the cool of the day (Genesis 3:8).

When sin infected the world, however, humanity turned from reflecting and living for God to worrying about what we wanted. This is fundamentally an issue of a lack of trust. When a child trusts a parent, they will do their homework and brush their teeth because they know that, in the long term, this will save them a lot of pain. They won't get detention or cavities tomorrow because they were obedient today. Most children don't learn this lesson right away, though. They want to eat what tastes sweet and do what feels good. They assume their parents just don't want them to have fun, and they may well have a wonderful time until the consequences meet them full in the face later.

Humanity turned from surrendering their free will to the laws of a good Father to using that same free will to honor our own desires. We valued our own wants and plans more than God's thoughts and ways. The conflict between human self-seeking and holy surrender is as old as time. We want to live our lives the way we see fit rather than listen to a heavenly killjoy who just doesn't understand. It often isn't until we see the big picture that we realize our error.

A self-seeking life is temporarily gratifying. It may relieve us to talk badly behind someone else's back or spend money like we are sultans. This results in tomorrow bringing fractured relationships and debts that we can't cancel. The stories in the Bible are powerful mosaics illustrating the consequences of self-seeking sin from Genesis to Revelation. A desire to taste what God had forbidden led to Adam and Eve's expulsion from the garden. They believed the lie that God was just holding out on them. Jealousy and pride resulted in Cain murdering his brother Abel. He couldn't accept that God didn't like his offering while his brother gained holy favor. Flagrant sinful acts culminated in humanity being wiped out by a flood. People thought Noah was nuts when he sported his rain boots that morning. Human hubris ultimately led to the dispersion of people and tongues when individuals tried to reach Heaven with the Tower of Babel. To this day, you can't visit most other countries without a translation app on your phone. Yet, Revelation is ultimately about God finally and fully saving us from our self-seeking demise.

Blessing in Pain

Mothers from all generations can tell you about the exquisite pain they suffered in childbirth, as well as the uncomfortable way their clothes fit for months. They can recall the food being launched at them by toddlers and the years they dreaded going to stores because of inevitable temper tantrums; they knew they would often be the targets of judgment. Yet, looking back, most would also tell you they would do it all again. When they place the graduation caps on their children's heads, they are often awe-struck that God has entrusted them with the incredible undertaking of raising the next generation. Parents know that none of it would have happened if they hadn't made the sacrifice.

Since the beginning of time, God has been working to bring people out of the pain, suffering, and destruction and back into the blessing He has for us through self-surrender. In modern times, we see powerful countries trying to devour those adjacent to them in regions like Europe and Asia. Individuals continue to cause pain and devastation due to their own desire for power and their need to see the self glorified. Yet, in the middle of the horror, neighboring countries are welcoming refugees, and people are being saved. God often shows His mercy in the most unlikely of places.

Because of His Son, we can repent and turn against our wicked ways, enjoying the free blessing of salvation. This great work started with one man named Abraham, and when God called him, He also gave him a promise of incredible blessing. Abraham would be the father of many nations, and his family would be eternally blessed by God. To this day, people of all nations who put their trust in God are considered children of Abraham. We are as numerous as the stars in the sky (Genesis 26:4), but what was first required of the patriarch? Self-surrender.

God told Abraham to leave his homeland, his dreams, and his plan for his life to surrender to the will of God. How many of us would travel to a different state or scrap our careers because God told us to? Very few, I imagine, yet what we see in Abraham's life is that the more he gave up, the more he gained from his heavenly Father. The opposite was true in Abraham's life as well. The more he took back the reigns and fell back into self seeking, the more trouble came his way. When he lied about his wife being his sister, he almost lost her to King Abimelech. Yet, God mercifully intervened before the king could touch her. One of Abraham's greatest acts of self-surrender came when he was willing to sacrifice his one and only son, Isaac, who carried the promise that God had given him. As a result, God spared Isaac, and the promise of blessing remained. His plan was a mystery to Abraham, but obedience brought favor he wasn't expecting.

Furthermore, with each character in the Old Testament, we see the same call of God. When people gave up their will, they were blessed. Moses gave up wealth in Egypt and was even willing to have his name removed from God's book of life if it meant saving his people, Israel. He delivered God's people from slavery and led them to the promised land. Daniel gave up certain foods and even power to be used for God's purposes. In the end, he was placed in authority over the wise men in Babylon. Shadrach, Meshach, and Abednego were willing to be thrown into a fire rather than worship someone besides their heavenly Father. It led to a nation falling on its knees before a Holy God. Esther was ready to give up her life to save her people, Israel. It resulted in the safety and celebration of God's people Israel when it looked as though they were doomed.

The truth that we see throughout the Bible is that blessing from God depends upon absolute surrender. The more we give up ourselves, the more we gain of God. Giving up is an art form because we know there are areas of our lives where we should be persistent and hold on and other areas where we must surrender our will to that of our Holy Father. This discernment is an art form. Like a painter or a sculptor, we must craft our time around this delicate balance of seeking our Father's will and doing our finest work with the tasks He has assigned us. Discerning the nuances requires patience, wisdom, and knowledge of His Word. There are times when it's appropriate to give up and times we should keep trying. When we aren't fulfilled in our physical or spiritual worlds, it's usually because we're holding onto things that we need to let go of. It's time to raise our little white flags and surrender to God so that we can experience what He has for us, which is so much better than what we would choose ourselves. What the Lord requires is just because He has presented us with the perfect example that we should follow.

The more we give up ourselves, the more we gain of God.

OUR MODEL FOR SELF-SURRENDER

Would you agree that the characters in the Old Testament who reflected God most radiantly were those who gave up the most? Were they also those who gained the most? If that is true, is it also true of those in the New Testament? Absolutely. In all counts, and primarily in the person and work of our Savior, Jesus Christ. As you will discover in this chapter, Jesus, bridging Old and New Testaments, is our prime example of enjoying the greatest blessing from God after making the greatest sacrifice.

Jesus Talks about Surrender

The language Jesus used throughout His life reflects the priority He placed on self-surrender. For example, in John 5:30, He said, "I can do nothing on my own. As I hear, I judge, and my judgment is just because I seek not my own will but the will of him who sent me." This is significant. Here the Savior of the World is stating He didn't come to Earth to do whatever made Him happy. Instead, He sought to do the will of His Father, who sent Him. How much more should we seek to be completely obedient to God?

Even from childhood, Jesus' life was one of total surrender to His heavenly Father. We all know plenty of pre-teens who think they are smarter than their parents, but Jesus actually was. Yet, He submitted to those in positions of authority over Him as an obedient child should. When He was twelve, He remained in Jerusalem after the Passover Festival, sitting with the teachers of scripture and asking them questions. Parents can identify with the dread that washes over them when they aren't sure where their child is for a moment. Jesus' mom and dad knew they were traveling with the Son of God, but they still panicked, frantically searching for Him. When they finally found Him, He was astounding those well-versed in the Law with His knowledge and wisdom. When asked where He had been, His answer was simply, "And He said to them, 'Why did you seek Me? Did you not know that I must be about My Father's business?'" (Luke 2:49, NJKV).

The language Jesus used throughout His life reflects the priority He placed on self-surrender.

Young Jesus considered the will of His Father in Heaven to be more important than that of anyone on Earth. Luke 2:51-52 also tells us, "[51] And he went down with them and came to Nazareth and was submissive to them. And his mother treasured up all these things in her heart. [52] And Jesus increased in wisdom and in stature and in favor with God and man." From this scripture, we see clearly that Jesus was an obedient child even as He continued to impress others with His knowledge of scripture and holy insights. His parents had to have been counting their blessings as they watched Him grow.

Throughout His lifetime, Jesus steadfastly continued with His practice of self-surrender. In John 14:10, He tells us, "Do you not believe that I am in the Father and the Father is in me? The words that I say to you I do not speak on my own authority, but the Father who dwells in me does his works." He continued to attribute His work on Earth to His self-surrender—His obedience to His Father in Heaven—refusing to speak on His own authority.

Later in the gospels, we see Jesus make the ultimate sacrifice by submitting to an excruciating death on the cross as a substitute for human sin. This clearly was not easy, as we see Him pleading with His Father on the night before His crucifixion: "And he said, 'Abba, Father, all things are possible for you. Remove this cup from me. Yet not what I will, but what you will'" (Mark 14:36). Jesus knew how difficult obedience would be and felt all the human emotions associated with this type of sacrifice: anguish, stress, and exhaustion.

In today's world, many view holy men as removed, perfect, and unfamiliar with pain, yet nothing could be further from the truth, as we see in our Savior's case. Jesus submitted to a sacrifice that makes what God asks from most of us look like a day counting shells on the beach. Even so, the perfect Son continued in His steadfast obedience.

If you're wondering what the blessings Jesus enjoyed were, allow me to list a few: He was Israel's ultimate rescuer from slavery. He was the ultimate prophetic voice of God, and the sacrificial Lamb offered up for sin once and for all. His reward is you and me when we receive eternal life with Him. He has also been given all authority in Heaven and on Earth, and the title King of Kings and Lord of Lords (Matthew 28:18, Revelation 19:16). Everything God desired for humanity was fulfilled in one Person and made possible through self-surrender.

11

So, where does that leave us? Speaking for myself—I'm a pastor. I'm not in the position of Abraham, Esther, or Daniel, who had to follow the sacrificial laws of the Old Testament. I'm also certainly not Jesus. Still, didn't He give up everything for me, so I don't have to pay the ultimate price for my sin? If Jesus had to submit to the will of the Father to gain the ultimate blessing for Himself and those He loves, why should I think I can complete His purpose for my life without self-surrender?

I know, I know. . . that is all valid and even borders on sounding pious, but how, exactly, do I surrender my own will to the Father's? Is there some kind of surrendering pill I can take to make me immediately humble and open to His will, no matter what it may entail? No, but what I call the Four C's of Self-Surrender will show us what scripture says about the matter.

The Four Cs of Self-Surrender

I like to think about self-surrender as the four Cs to make it easy to remember. The first of these is that Jesus *commands* it. As individuals, we are free to choose whether to follow Jesus. As Christians, however, we are not given the option of refusing to surrender to our Savior. In Luke 9:23-24, Jesus plainly stated, "[23] And he said to all, 'If anyone would come after me, let him deny himself and take up his cross daily and follow me. [24] For whoever would save his life will lose it, but whoever loses his life for my sake will save it.'"

As you can tell by now, self-denial is central to the Christian walk. We are told it's necessary if we wish to follow Him, yet the phrase "deny yourself," as we see it here, is the only time in the Bible such strong and overt language is used, aside from the story's parallels in Matthew and Mark. It's as if God knowingly and intentionally reserved such powerful language about surrendering oneself for this particular spiritual moment. Jesus has just foretold His own death on the cross, and He tells His disciples what it will take to follow Him—God's Son. The meaning of "deny" in Greek is powerful—the Greek word *arneomi*[1] is emphatic in its denial of the self as a person and not just things or ideas.

When people say yes to Heaven, often they're saying yes to fire insurance and they don't count the cost of following and submitting to Christ for the rest of their lives. Part of the problem is that we confuse becoming a Christian with simply saying "yes" to Heaven and "yes" to eternal life. But actually, becoming a Christian means saying "yes" to Jesus and "no" to self primarily. Your "yes" to Heaven is secondary and less important than your "yes" to and total surrender to Jesus. Luke 14:32 tells us "While the [king] is yet a great way off, he sends a delegation and asks for terms of peace." Only foolish people go up against a king that they can't defeat. Wise people count the cost and pursue peace before they face the King. There's a King we will face, and we don't want to go to war with him.

Your "yes" to Heaven is secondary and less important than your "yes" to and total surrender to Jesus.

When we say yes to Jesus, we're not just saying yes to him as our Savior, but also as our Lord. We're saying, "I'm surrendering Lordship over my life to you, Jesus." We're saying, "Jesus, your agenda as Lord, your plans as Lord, your desires, and ways, and truths, as Lord of my life are more important than my own. And again, this understanding of self-surrender is not optional if you want to be a follower of Jesus. Jesus commands self-surrender.

Good parents know the purpose of this. For example, we tell our children not to run into the street because we know an oncoming car could hurt them. Little ones may hear this command and become irritated that they can't do as they please, but we see things of which they aren't yet aware. As children mature, they will understand your wisdom and become thankful they had caring parents who made rules for their benefit. This is why Jesus commands self-surrender. He doesn't let us pick and choose which of His teachings to obey. He knows what is best for our long-term well-being, and He isn't going to allow us to wallow in the futility of our selfish desires.

The second C is that self-surrender is *contrary* to the ways of the world. A quick scroll through social media or a flip through Netflix libraries will show you that unselfishness is not popular. We don't see advertising appealing to our altruistic tendencies, or our humane desires to help others. Instead, ads pump us to the brim with our own egos. They tell us that if we drive a certain car or wear a particular brand, we can really show the world who we are. They promise we will have an attractive lifestyle and gain the ultimate reward according to them, which is the envy of everyone who knows us.

The lone fact that we have to *choose* self-surrender shows us that it's not natural for human beings. If left to our own devices, we will always choose ourselves rather than others. When children are born, they don't naturally share the things they love. In fact, if a sibling takes a toddler's toy, the little one will cry as though they've been robbed of every single thing they hold dear. Mature adults must teach the toddlers to share and take turns, which they find extremely disheartening at first.

In the same way, we often cannot see the ugliness of our selfishness the way others do, but Jesus can teach us how to put our brothers and sisters first. This may not be attractive to us initially, but it will ultimately make us into the types of people of whom the world will take notice.

The third C I want to highlight is that self-surrender is *costly.* What did Jesus mean when He said we must deny ourselves and take up our crosses if we want to follow Him (Luke 9:23)? Was He saying that we must carry actual wooden crosses on our backs to be genuine Christians? It may surprise you to know that for most of the original disciples, this was the case. In fact, all but one of the twelve disciples died martyrs' deaths for their faith. Still, is this kind of sacrifice required to follow Jesus? Often, no.

Many of us are blessed to live in nations where we are not physically persecuted because of what we believe…yet. What Jesus was letting us know here is that following Him is going to cost us something. It could be the material things you will give up by following Jesus into a career field that isn't known for its high pay. It could be the loss of social credit you suffer when others, including your own family and friends, ridicule you for your beliefs. It could mean you need to give up your dreams to follow God's plans for your life. As long as you're sure it is His will, the upside of surrendering your goals to those of your Savior is you will be blessed beyond your wildest imagination, but I will get to that in a bit.

The final C here is that self-surrender is *constant.* Luke 9:23 tells us to take up our crosses *daily.* This is not something we do once to get it over with. No, we have to commit each day to God's will. The apostle Paul says in 1 Corinthians 15:31b that " . . . I die every day!" Each morning, he would wake up and lay down His life for Christ and His ministry. He had a task of eternal significance: ministering and serving those His Savior cared for. He was willing to put aside his own priorities to achieve that end.

What many of us find frustrating is that our basic human selfishness doesn't disappear while we are on this Earth. We may achieve victory over addictions such as pornography or substance abuse, but we may never completely vanquish our temptations to indulge in these things. Those of us who are parents know that our children aren't going to turn into little saints just because they live in our homes. We must wake up every day with a commitment to love them and lead them to Jesus. The same holds true with our marriages and other relationships. They aren't going to become strong just because we want them to. We must begin each day with a commitment to serve, love, and surrender. The more we surrender, the more we will thrive.

Self-Surrender is Satisfying

Self-surrender is commanded, contrary, costly, and constant. This all sounds a bit difficult. And you know what? It is. That doesn't mean it isn't simple, though. If Jesus—the spotless Lamb of God—had to offer Himself as a sacrifice to save us, why should we, as imperfect, created beings, expect to live selfishly? Still, there is good news here. Jesus tells us in Luke 9:24 "For whoever would save his life will lose it, but whoever loses his life for my sake will save it." You cannot save yourself from yourself. Only Jesus can. So simply stop trying to rescue yourself and surrender to Jesus. When you lose your life to Him, He will save it. Moreover, the more you give up of yourself, the more you will gain of God. What happens when you gain more of God? I can assure you the benefits are too numerous to count, but I'll give you some examples shortly.

I understand some may be worried about losing their *identity* in the process of self-surrender. What about your personality, likes, and dislikes? You are a unique individual, and you don't want to turn into a robot who is just taking orders. Yet, that is why verse 24 is so important. When we surrender to Jesus, we don't lose ourselves. . . we discover our *true* selves. Your life will be saved. You will learn what it is to be truly human because you will be following the Perfect Human. What better identity than to be a co-heir of the Kingdom of God with Christ?

When we surrender to Jesus, we don't lose ourselves. . . we discover our true selves.

When you surrender yourself, you will live according to God's original and perfect intent before sin entered the world. Self-renunciation will lead to true self-realization in Christ. We will be amazed at what He can do through our earthly vessels. The dive-bar guitar player finds meaningful work as he leads thousands into worship through song on a Sunday morning. The workaholic becomes more present at home. The closed-handed person will begin donating their time and money freely. Those endlessly spinning their wheels to build their own kingdoms will suddenly begin to focus on others and the kingdom of God in their neighborhood, school, and workplace.

Surrendering ourselves to Christ in our work, our Christian communities, and our families makes life so much more satisfying. We are trusting the Creator, Sustainer, and King of the universe to take care of us. No one, not even ourselves, can take care of us the way Jesus can.

When you are a part of a community of believers that are surrendering themselves to Jesus, imagine the beautiful things that could happen! Is it possible for us to all put the needs of others above our own? Yes! Will it be difficult? Yes. But ultimately, it's worth a try.

What steps do you need to take to surrender yourself right now? In your heart, you know the truth. We cannot take the sacrifice of self-surrender lightly. Yet we also cannot underestimate its benefits. Where can you start today? Even in a small step. Your life will be saved when you give it up for Jesus' sake.

WHO'S ASKIN'?

I was in a Taco Bell drive-thru last week (don't judge). After I paid for my order, the cashier asked me if I wanted to give my change to charity. My first thought was, "Who's asking?" I knew the worker was asking me, but on whose behalf was she requesting money? If it was Planned Parenthood or some other "charity" whose values conflicted with my own, I wasn't going to give them my change, even if it was less than a dollar. As a rule, if I am going to give my money away, I want to make sure the organization will glorify God and truly help people.

Many of you remember a time when families had a house phone that was connected to a landline. We all shared it, but the adults of the home were usually given priority. (My parents still have one, even though the only people who ever call them are telemarketers). When we were younger, we were taught how to answer the family line properly: someone would call and say, "Is Mr. Eilert home?"

I wasn't supposed to just go get my dad. Instead, I was told to say, "Who's askin'?" Instead of using Mafioso verbiage, we stated it more politely, responding, "May I ask who's calling?" If the caller was someone my parents really didn't want to talk to or a scammer, I wouldn't have to bother my folks with the phone call. So, it was important to know who was asking before I passed the handset along. Not everyone was looking to swindle my parents out of money, and many callers were relatives or friends whom we loved and trusted, but my parents needed to know who was on the other side of the line before I could hand them the phone.

What we've learned so far is that the more we give up of ourselves, the more we gain of God. The more we live a life of surrender, sacrifice, and service to Him and others, the more satisfied we will be in all areas of life. The last thing we should do is hold onto something when true freedom only comes from giving up. Still, before we relinquish everything we've got, it helps to know who is asking us to make the sacrifice. (And God is completely fine with us asking the question).

The reason this works is that when we trust in someone's character and sincerity, we will be a lot more agreeable to doing as we're told. You may not, for example, be likely to give information like your Social Security number and bank account to a stranger who calls you up, promising you'll be paid back later. You would, however, be willing to pass along that sensitive information to a reputable company that has just hired you.

As we saw in Luke 9:23, Jesus our Savior demands complete surrender. "And he said to all, 'If anyone would come after me, let him deny himself and take up his cross daily and follow me.'" Giving up ourselves is not optional if we want to be followers of Christ, and that's a big ask.

Still, just as in other life scenarios, it's appropriate to find out, "Who's askin'?" We must have a track record with someone to know we can trust them not to hurt us with whatever we give them. If we don't have a relationship with an individual, we won't trust them. Why should we give up things we want so we can follow Jesus? What we must realize is we can trust God completely with our self-surrender. This makes the art of giving up so much easier. The question of "Who's askin'" is what makes it so difficult for many of us to trust God, yet, as we will see in this chapter, the answers will assure us that trusting Jesus is one of the safest things we can do.

God's Nature

What do you do when you find something valuable on the ground? You might be on your way to work and spot the glint of something polished out of the corner of your eye. When you realize it's jewelry, cash, or a cell phone, do you just walk away, thinking for a few seconds that it's too bad for the person who lost it? That's usually my response, but others think, "Finders, keepers!" and give themselves a little treat. My wife, Anette (from whom you'll hear in coming chapters of this book), is the only person I know who responds to this type of situation with great care and concern. She seems to have a special gift for noticing precious items lying around. Sometimes, we'll be walking in our neighborhood, and she'll spot a wallet, ring, or once, even a jacket in our path. Her immediate response is always dismay. She wants to get the valuable item back in the hands of its owner immediately. Thanks to her, many energetic toddlers have both shoes back on, and many grateful adults have their wallets back in their pockets or purses. She may have also saved a few households from some serious domestic squabbles!

The first person I think of when I consider a trustworthy individual is Annette. She takes honesty and integrity very seriously, even in "ordinary" situations. I never doubt she loves

21

and cares for me. When she says she will do something, she follows through, which is evidence of a rare and old-fashioned trait called "taking responsibility." She's not two-faced or hypocritical. She doesn't stand up against things in which she is secretly indulging behind closed doors. She doesn't lie, cheat, or steal. She doesn't treat people poorly, even when it would be easy to do so. She won't defame people when they aren't around. I know Annette isn't perfect. All of us fall short from time to time. Still, when I consider someone who is trustworthy, I immediately think of her.

Is there anyone in your life you can say you completely trust? Can you tell them secrets and know they will keep them? Do they have your best interests at heart when giving you advice? Do you know they will defend you when others are talking about you behind your back?

What if there was someone who met all your expectations of trustworthiness and remained completely without fault or sin? The truth is that it's in God's very nature to be trustworthy. Because we're all sinners, everyone in our lives will let us down at one time or another. All people are flawed works-in-progress, learning daily how to be honest, truthful, and faithful. By contrast, those traits aren't something that God needs to learn. They are already inherent in His Person. Once we know that God is perfect and always does what is right, we realize that He can be trusted.

Do you know any friends or family members you can trust to always be the standard of righteousness? Do you have a human ally who will never mess up, sin, or disappoint you? I can answer for you: no. Even so, we still manage to put our trust in some imperfect individuals, all the while struggling to put our faith in God. We'll discuss this struggle in more detail in the next chapter, but for now, I want us to focus on how it's in God's very nature to be trustworthy. Unlike our human confidants, we can lean on God completely and be certain He won't let us down.

Scripture gives us many ways to know that trusting in God is different from putting our faith in men and women. For example, Numbers 23:19 tells us that "God is not man, that he should lie, or a son of man, that he should change his mind. Has he said, and will he not do it? Or has he spoken, and will he not fulfill it?" We all know what it's like to have someone say that they will do something and have them disappoint us. Some of us have even been in the position of not keeping our word! By contrast, this scripture is letting us know that God is not like that. When He says He will do something, we should consider it done. He is not like our human counterparts, prone to making promises they can't keep.

Similarly, Psalms 18:30 tells us, "This God—his way is perfect; the word of the Lord proves true; he is a shield for all those who take refuge in him." Babies need to take refuge in their parents to have their basic needs met. They are helpless to feed or clothe themselves. Their only choice is to trust that their parents will do as they promise and take care of them. In the same way, we can take refuge in the Word of the Lord. No matter what happens while we are on this Earth, we know that His promises will meet their fulfillment when the time is right.

We can also look at Lamentations 3:22-23, which tells us that "[22] The steadfast love of the Lord never ceases; his mercies never come to an end; [23] they are new every morning; great is your faithfulness." We can count on the Lord's love never to end. In fact, His mercies, or His kindness and compassion toward us, are new every morning! That means each day, we can wake up and wonder how He will forgive us and surprise us with His love. Did you open your eyes today to discover harsh punishment for your sin or to a glorious sunrise that you didn't deserve to see? God's limitless power and steadfast love demonstrate complete faithfulness. This is so different from the broken love we often experience in human relationships.

Show and Tell

Because it's His nature, we can trust God to be trustworthy. And if you know anything about logic or are an aspiring logician like me, you realize that this is a circular argument. That means that you're starting with the statement with which you want to end. Circular arguments aren't very convincing. It's like saying that eighteen-year-olds should have the right to vote because it's legal for them to do so or that we shouldn't break the law because it's illegal. The law in itself is not enough of a reason to follow it. It could be an unjust or discriminatory rule that we are asking people to obey. Circular arguments simply aren't convincing.

People often use circular reasoning when they don't want to do the work to prove that what they are saying is correct. Insisting that we should trust God because He is trustworthy is an example of this. Still, if we do the work, we will find that God shows us He is trustworthy by the way He uses His power and strength, not to serve Himself, but to benefit us. This is exemplified in Jesus' total self-surrender on the cross for us. There's a reason why John 3:16 is the most popular verse in the Bible: "For God so loved the world, that he gave his only Son, that whoever believes in him should not perish but have eternal life." God showed us His power and love through His sacrifice and provision when He didn't have to intervene.

We can also look at the promises that God fulfilled. For example, in Genesis 17, God promised Abraham that he would be the father of many nations. Despite the delay and Abraham's impatience, God kept His promise. To this day, the children of Abraham are all of those who trust in Christ and follow Him out of obedience in faith. We are countless. All those who have faith in Christ are Abraham's descendants and heirs of the covenant promises.

That wasn't the only set of promises God fulfilled. He kept His Word by leading the Israelites through the wilderness and parting the Red Sea. He brought them out of exile and back into

Jerusalem. He promised King David that one of his descendants would build God's Holy Temple, and his son Solomon did just that. Throughout the Old Testament, God promised a Messiah would come into the world to save it, and just when it seemed that God had forgotten about His people, Jesus was born. In fact, over 100 prophecies that were made in the Old Testament 400-1,500 years before Jesus' birth were fulfilled in His Person. It's estimated the chance of a man living in modern times and fulfilling just eight of the clearest prophecies about the Messiah in the Old Testament is one in 100,000,000,000,000,000.[2] There's a much better chance that I will win the Mega Millions! I think it takes more faith *not* to believe that Jesus is the Messiah than to embrace His deity.

God is a show-and-tell God.

The Bible tells us in 2 Corinthians 1:20, "For all the promises of God find their Yes in him. That is why it is through him that we utter our Amen to God for his glory." God's promises aren't always fulfilled when we think they should be, but He will always do as He said He would. That's what sets His love apart.

The bottom line is that God is a show-and-tell God. He doesn't have to prove His trustworthiness, but I'm happy that He does. The demonstration of His trustworthiness isn't for His own sake but ours. Many of the Psalms talk about how, once we put our trust in God, blessings follow. For example, Psalms 37:3-6 tells us to

> [3] Trust in the Lord, and do good; dwell in the land and befriend faithfulness.
>
> [4] Delight yourself in the Lord, and he will give you the desires of your heart.
>
> [5] Commit your way to the Lord; trust in him, and he will act.
>
> [6] He will bring forth your righteousness as the light, and your justice as the noonday.

Here, we see that when we trust in God and do what is right, He will act on our behalf. He will make the righteousness of our cause shine like the sun in the middle of the day. When we commit to a life of integrity, He will make our righteousness radiate before men. When God's love and law are the delights of our hearts, we will find our desires fulfilled because they will be in line with His own.

Still, when we hear the call to total self-surrender, it's normal to want to know, "Who's askin'?" We shouldn't be afraid of honest questioning. It will lead us to a God who has proven His trustworthiness time and again. As when a trusted friend or family member has asked something of us, we are happy to oblige because that individual has proven themselves trustworthy. Surrendering is an art that becomes much easier once we realize to whom we are surrendering. He is the only Person worthy of complete and refreshing surrender.

WHY THE
STRUGGLE?

A s I mentioned in the last chapter, my wife Annette does
things like return lost bracelets to complete strangers. I
don't struggle to trust her. I don't have to stir up faith by
repeating incantations or singing love songs before I talk to her. I
don't bite my nails all afternoon, wondering if she will keep her
promises to me. Over the years, we've done the continual work
of getting to know each other. I am aware of Annette's strengths
and weaknesses, and I know that she will keep her word.

Many of us understand on some level that God is trustworthy.
Scripture tells us that He alone is uniquely qualified to be the Lord
of the Universe and our hearts. Still, many Christians struggle to
trust Him. Why do we see clear guidance in scripture yet do the
opposite of what it tells us? Why do we grapple with letting go

of the reigns and allowing Him to be the Lord and Master of our lives?

I believe there are three main reasons why we find it so difficult. These reasons have plagued us at one time or another, but many of us have never challenged them. Overcoming our obstacles to faith could be the difference between a life of fulfilling surrender and one of empty religious drudgery.

Three Reasons We Struggle to Trust God

It may not be popular to talk about in modern times, but one of the main reasons individuals struggle to trust God is old-fashioned, garden-variety pride. We think we know better. When it comes to human relationships, we guard ourselves carefully. I know I am the only one who knows my personality, including my likes, dislikes, dreams, and goals. I know what I'm capable of and what I'm unable to do. Why should I trust someone else to tell me what my future should be? These attitudes result in having trouble trusting our Savior as well as other people.

It isn't easy to trust others, especially regarding things like our plans. How can we ensure they won't discourage us or shatter our hopes? What if they tell us to become something we don't want to be? Many individuals have controlling parents or nosy friends. In many cases, it's best not to share our most cherished aspirations with them. They will have their own agendas and may even seek to do us harm.

Despite the poor examples we see on Earth, I want to assure you that this is not the case with your heavenly Father. He isn't looking to trap you with His laws. He doesn't view you as a puppet or aim to make Himself look good at your expense. In fact, we learn in Luke 12:7 that He knows the number of hairs on your head. Jeremiah 29:11 tells us, "For I know the plans I have for you, declares the Lord, plans for welfare and not for evil, to give you a future and a hope." God knows what's ahead of you, including tomorrow's coffee spills, next Tuesday's weather forecast, and who will live in your neighborhood three centuries from now, but do you know the future? Even when you make plans, can you guarantee that you will be able to see them through?

Psalms 139:13 reminds us, "For you formed my inward parts; you knitted me together in my mother's womb." Can you think of anyone else who knew you while you were a sprouting baby in your mother's belly? Can any other person recall what it was like to watch you grow toes? God knows you better than anyone else, but He also knows you better than you know yourself. We all have skills and aspirations, and we don't have them by accident. Still,

God knows you better than anyone else, but He also knows you better than you know yourself.

your plans may not be the best blueprint for your life. God knows things even if you don't know about your disposition and circumstances. When you surrender to God's will, you may quickly discover a purpose that gives your life new meaning.

King Solomon was the wisest man in scripture next to Jesus. When God offered to grant this son of King David any request, he asked for wisdom (1 Kings 3:9). God was so pleased with this response that He lavished on Solomon abundant insight, along with the riches and honor he hadn't asked for (1 Kings 3:12-13). And wise, discerning King Solomon tells us in Proverbs 3:5-6 to "⁵ Trust in the Lord with all your heart and lean not on your own understanding; ⁶ in all your ways submit to him, and he will make your paths straight." It takes true wisdom to realize that we shouldn't rely on our experiences, knowledge, or desires. Instead, we can trust in Him. He flat-out knows better than us in every situation.

The second reason why I believe we often struggle to trust in God is that we don't know Him well. As I mentioned at the chapter's beginning, my familiarity with my wife is what leads me to trust her. Close relationships take work. That may require counseling, reading books together, or sharing our deepest fears. Once we have done this, we can begin to trust that our spouse is truly in our corner, always rooting for us, even if they don't express it flawlessly. All of us are imperfect, but building trust requires a sincere effort. Similarly, you won't be able to trust in a God you don't know. This isn't because He hasn't revealed His nature and character to us; we saw in Chapter 3 that He had done this quite clearly. Rather, we haven't worked on our relationship enough to build intimacy and really get to know Him.

The more you know about God and what He's done for you, the more you will trust Him.

The more you know about God and what He's done for you, the more you will trust Him. I love what Psalms 9:10 tells us: "And those who know your name put their trust in you, for you, O Lord, have not forsaken those who seek you." The people who know God best realize that He has never forsaken them. The more we know Him, the more we will trust Him.

The third reason why I believe most people don't trust in God is that we don't practice trust in Him. Living a life without any friends or family you trust is miserable. Still, to trust, you must take a risk in getting to know an imperfect person, someone who could break your trust or hurt you somehow. The solution is usually to trust the other individual with something small to allow them to prove their trustworthiness. Gradually, you can entrust them with more and more of your heart. Once real trust has been established, your life will begin to flourish in the soil of a healthy relationship.

The same is true in our relationship with God, with one important distinction: God's love is perfect and trustworthy in every way. Ideally, we will recognize from evidence in scripture and our own lives that God is completely trustworthy, and everything He does is for our ultimate good. Still, we continue to struggle with trust.

Some of us would like to say "I trust you" over and over to God, like a mantra, and eventually have our statement become true. Yet we can't just speak it and expect it to materialize; we have to demonstrate trust. Like our human relationships, I believe it's okay to begin trusting God with the small things. Young musicians don't play Mozart or Bach because they say that's what they want to do. Rather, they practice simpler exercises and folk songs over and over until they develop the skills they need to dazzle on something more difficult. In the same way, it takes practice with basic disciplines to become a person of deep faith.

Growing Trust

Think for a moment about a day you started a new class at school. You were a little nervous and may not have realized that your teacher was, too. Still, a student rarely raises their hand and asks their instructor to prove their credentials before they begin to listen. Rather, you followed class rules, and the educator earned your esteem by imparting knowledge and helping you develop important skills.

In the same way, trusting God is an on-the-way process. God's word tells us, "The earth produces by itself, first the blade, then the ear, then the full grain in the ear" (Mark 4:28). Growth happens in stages, and maturity takes time. Many of the disciples didn't believe that Jesus was the Messiah immediately, but that didn't stop them from trusting Him. Most didn't ask Him for proof of His divinity before they began to obey. When Jesus said to follow Him, they dropped what they were doing and accompanied Him, eventually trusting that He was, in fact, the Messiah for Whom they had been waiting.

Once you say "yes" to Jesus, He will prove Himself faithful. One of the most practical ways to grow our trust in God is to read scripture, which is an exercise in trust. It's thousands of years old, and sometimes it may not be easy to understand. This is where resources like concordances, reliable websites, or knowledgeable folks in your church can help you to make sense of it. When you read scripture, even when you don't feel like it, you take a powerful step in faith. In 2 Timothy 3:14-17, Paul encourages Timothy:

Trusting God is an on-the-way process.

[14] But as for you, continue in what you have learned and have firmly believed, knowing from whom you learned it [15] and how from childhood you have been acquainted with the sacred writings, which are able to make you wise for salvation through faith in Christ Jesus. [16] All Scripture is breathed out by God and profitable for teaching, for reproof, for correction, and for training in righteousness, [17] that the man of God may be complete, equipped for every good work.

Paul commended Timothy for his knowledge of scripture, which was why the young man's faith was so strong. You'll get to know God's heart when you immerse yourself in His Word. Scriptures make us wise; they are the rock-solid reason we can denounce certain behaviors and applaud others. If you are a Christian who feels weak, a deeper knowledge of scripture can put your feet on solid ground. It will bring you from doubting God to trusting Him. In John 17:17 Jesus asks God, "Sanctify them in the truth; your word is truth." The "sanctifying" Jesus requests is being transformed into His likeness, who put His full faith and trust in God. Another critical way to trust in God is through prayer. When your heart experiences overwhelming joy or pain, who do you turn to? Can anyone understand us the way our heavenly Father does? In Psalms 3:4, King David says, "I cried aloud to the Lord, and he answered me from his holy hill. Selah" If you pray and the infinite God who created and sustains the universe answers you, who are imperfect and finite, you have a splendid reason to trust him. Of course, He may not always answer the way we want Him to, and we can actually be thankful for that.

A third way we can practice trust is through praise and worship. Again, scripture illustrates this, such as when the Holy Spirit (through Jahaziel) told King Jehoshaphat to worship rather than fight an approaching enemy (2 Chronicles 20). The Lord told Him that "the battle is not yours but God's" (2 Chronicles 20:15b). As an enormous army approached, the men in Israel's camp laid down their weapons, fell to their knees, and worshipped. Put yourself in the shoes of one of the Israelite soldiers. Would you have trusted God enough to respond the way they did, knowing the enemy that was advancing toward you? And yet, while they were praising, God sent an angel to wipe out the adversaries of His people. First, however, they needed to respond in obedience.

I can't tell you the number of times I've worried and stressed myself to pieces about the problems in my life. When I finally surrendered to God, He calmed my heart, soul, and mind. I remembered who He is through praise and worship and how He has blessed me so far. I know many of you have similar stories. The prophet Habakkuk sang

[17] Though the fig tree should not blossom, nor fruit be on the vines, the produce of the olive fail and the fields yield no food, the flock be cut off from the fold and there be no herd in the stalls,
[18] yet I will rejoice in the Lord; I will take joy in the God of my salvation.
[19] God, the Lord, is my strength; he makes my feet like the deer's; he makes me tread on my high places. Habakkuk 3:17-19

The power of prayer is amplified when the enemy tells us that God has abandoned us and our circumstances seem to confirm the lie. When we praise and worship during those times, it's an act of obedience that requires a great deal of discipline. Moreover, God's power increases exponentially.

Another way Christians can practice trust is through tithing. Malachi 3:10-12 tells us to

> [10] Bring the full tithe into the storehouse, that there may be food in my house. And thereby put me to the test, says the Lord of hosts, if I will not open the windows of heaven for you and pour down for you a blessing until there is no more need. [11] I will rebuke the devourer for you, so that it will not destroy the fruits of your soil, and your vine in the field shall not fail to bear, says the Lord of hosts. [12] Then all nations will call you blessed, for you will be a land of delight, says the Lord of hosts.

Tithing is a simple exercise by which we give ten percent of our earnings to the Lord of Hosts, who provided us with everything we have. I have heard many stories from those in my congregation who initially told me what a sacrifice tithing was, but they always saw God's faithfulness revealed in time.

Finally, we can trust God by following the promptings of His Holy Spirit. If you're a follower of Jesus, you have His Spirit living inside you. He is your Helper in life, and He is watching over you right now. Sometimes He will offer you wisdom beyond your years. Other times His touch will look like healing, deliverance, or courage in the face of adversity. Yet often, you will feel a slight nudge to go left instead of right. The Holy Spirit will point you to pray for someone or give money to a friend who needs it. This happened to me when I didn't understand why I was prodded to do something. In the end, God used it to bless me in ways I could never have imagined.

Trust is not conceptual; it is practical. Saying you trust won't make you a trusting person. Instead, you'll need to practice it, and God will return your faithfulness by proving His trustworthiness. Does self-surrender seem like a difficult thing to do? Maybe that's because you need to know the Person you're trusting better. You will discover that God's trustworthiness isn't solely for His sake but also our blessing and favor.

Psalms 33:20-22 says, "[20] Our soul waits for the Lord; he is our help and our shield. [21] For our heart is glad in him, because we trust in his holy name. [22] Let your steadfast love, O Lord, be upon us, even as we hope in you." When your heart is glad in the faithfulness of your God, your struggle will transform into a joyful offering.

TAKE IT OFF

In the past few chapters, we've looked deeply into what it means to live a life of sacrifice, surrender, and service. If a person wants to follow Jesus, relinquishing her will to His is not optional. We've also discovered that the Person asking for our sacrifice is a loving, perfect, and trustworthy God. We can trust Him with our self-surrender because the more we trust Him, the easier the art of surrender becomes.

We never want to be in a place where we hold onto things we should give up and give up things onto which we should hold. This is a formula for misery. Still, how do we know when to hold tightly to something and when it's time to let it go? We could easily flip the book's title and call it "The Art of Holding On." There are times in the Christian walk when we are called to stay the course even though it's painful simply because our heavenly Father told us to do so. This is because God wants more for our marriages, careers, and community lives. Our heavenly Father doesn't just want our lives to be good; He wants them to be great! Still, something holds us back. We need to know when to give up and when to hold on. I'm here to tell you that it's time to take it off!

Naturally Good

Merriam-Webster's dictionary defines an art form as a "form or medium of expression recognized as fine art."[3] When I think about art forms, I immediately think back to my junior high, high school, and college years as a trumpeter. I originally wanted to play the saxophone, but the band director said he had a feeling the trumpet would be a better fit. As it turned out, he was right! Even as a sixth grader, I had a natural ability on the instrument and an instinctive ear for pitches and rhythms. I became the first chair in my elementary school band's trumpet section and the lead trumpeter in my junior high band. I was the first chair trumpet player in high school, too. When I got to college, I didn't sit in the first chair, but I was always at the top of the section with the juniors and seniors. My band directors could all see that I had quite a natural gift. But I had one major flaw. All of my ensemble directors discovered they couldn't rely on me for solos.

I was a great ensemble musician and loved playing with the rest of the band. Still, when I was given a solo, as first-chair trumpet players often are, I couldn't do it. I messed up during live performances in front of audiences, which were the moments when playing the score correctly mattered the most. Even more frustrating was that I knew what the problem was, and my directors knew as well–I didn't practice! I relied too heavily on my natural abilities and wasn't willing to put in the extra effort.

While I could work quite hard with the rest of the band during rehearsal time, I was unwilling to spend much time alone in a practice room. All of my band directors agreed that, while I was a good trumpet player, I needed to start practicing if I wanted to be great. Unfortunately, I didn't listen to them. I coasted on the waves of my natural ability throughout elementary, junior high, high school, and college. I gave up on the fundamentals of practice, like boring scales and etudes. Because I held onto what I should have given up (relying solely on my natural ability) and gave up what I should have held onto (hours in the practice room), I struggled to become a great trumpet player. My band directors had no choice but to give the opportunities to players who actually practiced.

When it comes to areas like the arts and athletics, we all know "greats" we'd love to emulate. The truth is that all of the exceptional musicians, artists, cooks, actors, and writers that you know have something in common. They all reached a point when they could no longer rely upon natural talent, which would only take them so far. It was time to discipline themselves, practice, and hone their skills. Without constant repetition and improvement, they would never have been able to break records or dazzle audiences. So they toiled over difficult measures on their instrument until they played them flawlessly. Or they rehearsed their lines until they could say them without thinking. Or they read works by great authors, studying their use of language until they developed a compelling voice of their own.

Scripture tells us, "Do not be deceived: God is not mocked, for whatever one sows, that will he also reap" (Galatians 6:7). God sees the effort we are putting in, and He will reward us according to it. We may be able to get away with minimal work for a while, but our lack of effort will eventually catch up with us. This is true regarding rudimentary disciplines such as practicing an instrument, but it's also vital in our relationships with others. We will receive compassion in return if we think and behave in ways full of mercy and grace. On the other hand, if we sow selfishness and act harshly with our friends and family, we should not expect others to shower us with empathy.

Have you ever found yourself at a crossroads, knowing you had to use your time more wisely if you wanted to become greater? Maybe the problem is that you've surrendered what was best in exchange for what was secondary. Ephesians 3:20 tells us, "Now to him who is able to do far more abundantly than all that we ask or think, according to the power at work within us." When you surrender to your heavenly Father, you will be amazed at what he can do with your earthly vessel. It may even be something of which you've never dreamed. But first, you have to take it off.

No Good

Natural ability can take you a certain distance. You may even get "discovered" by someone, such as a sports recruiter or a record producer. Still, these professionals aren't going to invest time and money in someone who is just good. They will expect you to be great. This requires an old-fashioned concept called discipline, which involves putting off something you'd like to do now with the hope of gaining something in the future. For some folks, this may include hours at the gym. For others, it will mean slogging through difficult classes to earn a degree. Still, other individuals will need to learn how to get along with individuals they don't like because they are striving for a promotion at work. We all need to sacrifice and endure painful moments to get where we want to be. The good news is that it won't go unrewarded if we continue in faith and obedience.

Similarly, natural ability alone won't cut it in our walks with Jesus. Human nature, in its natural state, is selfish and sinful. We tend to put ourselves above others, known in the Bible as the "old self" or the "old creation." Scripture doesn't celebrate this natural tendency. In fact, it tells us that it will lead to death (Romans 8:13). In Ephesians 4:22-24, the apostle Paul tells us we should strive "[22] to put off your old self, which belongs to your former manner of life and is corrupt through deceitful desires, [23] and to be renewed in the spirit of your minds, [24] and to put on the new self, created after the likeness of God in true righteousness and holiness."

Our job as Christians is to constantly put off our selfish pleasures and desires to gain something more significant, which is likeness to God in righteousness and holiness. What an incredible promise! Our heavenly Father wants us to be just like Him in how good and pleasing we are to those that meet us. We can be a splash of rain on a summer day, but only if we surrender.

Romans 3:10-12 tells us, "[10] as it is written: 'None is righteous, no, not one; [11] no one understands; no one seeks for God. [12] All have turned aside; together they have become worthless; no one does good, not even one.'" Here, the writer is quoting Psalms 14 and 53. Even during Old Testament times, holy men agreed with God that no one on Earth was good and righteous in their own strength. Everyone has gone astray and sought their own glory, pleasures, and desires.

In Mark 10:18b, Jesus asked, "Why do you call me good? No one is good except God alone." Our Savior is reminding us that no teacher is good in their nature; God alone is holy all the time. When it comes to experiencing a great and satisfying life with God, we have nothing with which to start. There is no natural human inclination toward goodness or holiness.

You may now be thinking, "Wow, what an encouraging message! I'm so glad I picked up this book! It's wonderful to know that I am not good or holy and will never please God in my own nature." Individuals who have striven to earn Heaven through their works may find it discouraging to realize that The Holy One will never find them acceptable. Yet the good news is, while that's where our story finds us, it's not where it ends. I believe this is a positive message in the end.

Something Great

Understanding our innate sinfulness is encouraging once we see how our Savior rescues us. Our surrender allows us to give up trying to be holy in our own power. We can finally accept that we are, in fact, hopelessly flawed and selfish. We won't be tempted, like teenaged Pastor Kai, to hold on to our natural abilities and trust that they will get us places. We can imagine Jesus saying, "Hey, give up your striving. Take off that old self, and I will give you something greater. Your old self is no good." So, when our Savior gives us this freedom, why don't believers just do it? We'll take a closer look at why in the next chapter.

You may think you know all that Jesus expects us to surrender to Him, but you're going to have to open your Bible to get a better idea of what he's talking about. Ephesians 4:25-30 tells us:

> [25] Therefore, having put away falsehood, let each one of you speak the truth with his neighbor, for we are members one of another. [26] Be angry and do not sin; do not let the sun go down on your anger, [27] and give no opportunity to the devil. [28] Let the thief no longer steal, but rather let him labor, doing honest work with his own hands, so that he may have something to share with anyone in need. [29] Let no corrupting talk come out of your mouths, but only such as is good for building up, as fits the occasion, that it may give grace to those who hear. [30] And do not grieve the Holy Spirit of God, by whom you were sealed for the day of redemption.

Some of the things the writer, Paul, tells us to do may seem obvious. For example, we shouldn't steal; instead, we should find something useful and productive to do with our time so that we have enough to share with those in need. This is a strong admonishment for those Christians who tend to waste time on social media or goof off. We need to pull our own weight and make the world a better place through our generosity. God will hold us accountable for the use of these resources one day.

Furthermore, most of us know we shouldn't lie. Still, Paul is also cautioning us against unwholesome talk, which may be tempting for Christians when hanging out with unsaved or even Christian friends in casual settings. Using unsavory language may seem natural, and we don't want to appear pious or inapproachable. Yet a positive Christian witness requires us to take it off. He also reminds us to build others up according to their needs. When we see someone who seems insecure or heartbroken, do we build up their sense of self-worth? Do we reach out to provide physical assistance for those without food or shelter? Do we warn those who are idle? Living a life of surrender means exchanging coarse chatter for encouraging expressions. The Bible warns us that "Death and life are in the power of the tongue, and those who love it will eat its fruits" (Proverbs 18:21). We can use our words to build others up or tear them down, but we can be certain we will reap what we sow.

We are also told that, while it isn't a sin to be angry, we are not to lash out at others in our frustration. This will give the devil a foothold or a secure place from which he can influence our actions and the relationships with those we love. The next time you're angry, you can please your heavenly Father by holding your tongue and waiting until your emotions have stopped boiling to respond. Find healthy ways to deal with what your heart is telling you, such as journaling or praying. Then, respond with love and patience if the issue needs to be addressed. Your immediate family, as well as your church family, will benefit immensely from this response. In addition, we're reminded not to grieve the Holy Spirit of God. We must put off actions that hinder His work in our lives, thus causing Him pain and distress. We shouldn't ignore His promptings to be kind or holy. Instead, we can clothe ourselves in righteousness and forgiveness toward those who offend us.

As you read through this list, you may realize that you're donning garb that doesn't please your heavenly Father. To live a successful life, you must take it off! Put away bitterness, anger, clamor, and slander. These are attitudes no Christians should be cultivating in their hearts. No one is perfect, and we will all fall sometimes. Remember that those are moments when you can repent, turn from your ways, and keep moving forward. Surrendering is, above all, an art. Like any other craft, your mistakes can be turned into masterpieces if you turn to the correct Source.

At the beginning of this chapter I briefly touched on how we should know when to hold onto something and when to release something. The next chapter will help you gain a much clearer understanding of how to discern this wisdom.

GREAT POSSESSIONS

What do you have that you consider a great possession? Do you have a house you've worked hard for or a perfect car for your family? Are you the proud owner of a fine antique jewelry collection? Do your friends envy your baseball card binders or salivate over your wardrobe?

All of us have possessions we consider great. For some, it could be a high-paying job. Money isn't a concern for you. Others take pride in their non-tangible possessions, such as a career choice, identity, or fine reputation. Maybe you're holding tightly to your career goals, trusting that the future will be better than the present. Or perhaps what you value is the past and your "good ol' days" experiences? We all have great possessions in some form or another, and holding onto them isn't a sin. Still, when we hold onto things God calls us to give up, we truly are being sinful (James 4:17). This is a formula for dissatisfaction in life.

Lacking One Thing

In Mark 10:18, Jesus pointed out that no one was good except God alone. Now we will look at a biblical character who walked the straight and narrow, lived a respectable life, and followed God's way as best he could. In that sense, he had already shed his old self and was living as a new man. Yet, he was still holding onto something that kept him from experiencing all God had planned. Let's look at Mark 10:17-20:

> [17] And as he was setting out on his journey, a man ran up and knelt before him and asked him, "Good Teacher, what must I do to inherit eternal life?" [18] And Jesus said to him, "Why do you call me good? No one is good except God alone. [19] You know the commandments: 'Do not murder, Do not commit adultery, Do not steal, Do not bear false witness, Do not defraud, Honor your father and mother.'" [20] And he said to him, "Teacher, all these I have kept from my youth."

There are a couple of important things to note here. First, this man obviously respects Jesus and believes He is at least a man of God. He kneels before Him, which is a posture of humility and respect. Furthermore, he has given up a sinful life and begun seeking God and His ways. It appears he has surrendered what he should surrender and held onto what was true. I must admit that if this man were in my congregation today, I would think he was a good guy. I would make him a small group leader. Some of the single ladies might even take an interest in him. No one would question whether he was a believer. Many of us would be proud to live the same way. We would pat ourselves on the back for living a pretty good life. Still, Jesus withholds the pat on the back, at least for now. We read in verses 21 and 22:

> [21] And Jesus, looking at him, loved him, and said to him, "You lack one thing: go, sell all that you have and give to the poor, and you will have treasure in heaven; and come, follow me." [22] Disheartened by the saying, he went away sorrowful, for he had great possessions.

This man was doing well, but there was one thing he still needed to experience a truly great life. At this moment, he holds onto something that Jesus calls him to give up. He walks away sorrowful and dissatisfied. What Jesus asks him to give up isn't overtly sinful; this man isn't living according to his old nature. Still, he isn't surrendering everything he is supposed to.

Placing value on your physical possessions, job, or status isn't sinful. We read in 1 Thessalonians 3:10, "For even when we were with you, we would give you this command: If anyone is not willing to work, let him not eat." God doesn't want us to be idle. As we learned in the last chapter, God expects us to stay busy with the work He has given us so that we have something to give those in need. It's also not wrong to have dreams and goals. Many of us find that healthy, unselfish plans are what keep our minds from wallowing in cesspools of sin. In addition, it isn't wrong to look back on the past and evaluate its merits and mistakes to build a better future. Still, there are times when God might ask you to give up a great possession for the sake of surrendering to His calling. At that moment, we need to make an evaluation. Do we hold onto that precious thing or give it up to Him? Moreover, how do we know when Jesus calls us to surrender something important to Him? We'll explore that later in the chapter.

There are times when God might ask you to give up a great possession for the sake of surrendering to His calling.

There's also the question of why Jesus would ask us to give up something when there is no harm in keeping it. The man in the story walked away sorrowfully. That's because, even though he was wealthy and lacked no earthly thing, he still wasn't satisfied. None of us wants to be there. God desires that we will give up something good to gain what is great. If God asks you to give up something precious, it's because He has something greater in store for you. That's what God promised this man. He would have treasure in Heaven! That kind of fortune is eternal and cannot be destroyed by moths, rust, or fire.

And we know things that the rich young ruler didn't. If he had given up his riches to follow Jesus, he would have witnessed miracles, healings, deliverances, and resurrections. He would have been a part of the greatest movement the world has ever seen, one with an impact that will last into eternity. Instead, he held himself back by clinging to what he should have given up. He missed out on something greater. When we hold onto what we believe will bring us happiness, we often relinquish the thing that could end up filling us with peace and joy. Don't hold onto what God tells you to give up.

Draw or Distract

Sometimes, the art of giving up can be more subtle than a direct choice spelled out for us by our Savior. One of the most challenging things about surrendering is knowing when God is really calling you to surrender and when you are simply experiencing a prompting from your own heart. Other influences, such as relatives or spouses, can also cause us to doubt whether God is truly encouraging us to do something. Sometimes, the source of the prompting is obvious. If you feel led to stop sinning, the Holy Spirit is probably talking. Still, there are times when we just aren't sure.

One consideration is whether the pursuit in question will draw you closer to God or distract you from Him. Will it lead you to a more profound knowledge of God and allow you to fulfill His greater purpose for your life? You should probably hold onto it. Will it distract you from living the life God has called you to live? Then it probably pays to give it up and take it off.

This is a personal decision since the earthly activities that distract will vary from person to person. For example, you may be able to have games and news apps on your phone, but I just can't. There's nothing wrong with those, but I find them to be a tremendous drain on my time. Once I find a game I'm good at or see an intriguing morning headline, I'm sucked into the vortex of wanting more. The addicting applications chip away at the precious time I could spend on my work or family. I had to do another phone purge recently because I'd convinced myself I'd be okay this time. But nope! I don't know what it is about those apps that so easily distract me, but the only way to avoid the catnip is to keep it out of the house. Without those distractions, I live a deeper, more satisfying life. I can draw closer to God and freely pursue His purpose.

Your distraction may be different from mine. Maybe you're easily pulled into gossip, social media, or snacks. Perhaps when you see your coworker walking by, or an email pops up on your phone, you know you're going to be pulled away from your career, family, or volunteer work for a while. In times like those, you must let your faith goals win over your natural impulses. Do you want to start a new ministry, be a good witness to your family, or read an encouraging book? Is your goal to grow closer to God so you can trust Him more? Then you'll need to give up the things that hold you back.

If your possessions distract you from your life of surrender to Jesus, it's time to ditch them, give them up, and take them off, no matter how small or silly they may seem. So put your cell phone in a drawer the next time you're having a family dinner. Tell the gossipy lady in the next cubicle that you're too busy to talk. Don't buy cookies at the store because you know your church and family need you to be healthy. On the other hand, feel free to put on those pursuits that move you closer to your faith goal. Make sure surrendering will draw you into God's kingdom rather than distract you from its work.

Don't Give Up

We've talked about letting go of things that aren't good for us, but what about giving up on the things we should be clinging to? I think that sometimes we get to a point in life where we become loose with the fundamentals of our faith. This relates to the dependence on a natural ability I mentioned at the beginning of the chapter. We start to rely on ourselves, our own strength, and our ability to live a good life. This self-reliance can creep in during different seasons for different people. Some start to hold onto themselves when life gets hard. They decide they need to hunker down, stay strong, and get through it. It happens when life is going well, and things seem easy for others. They feel like they've got it and can take things from here. Thanks anyway, God!

When we're in that self-reliant place, I believe there are three things we give up. We don't leave our faith altogether but relinquish vital aspects that lead to a truly satisfying life. Ironically enough, they all start with a C. We tend to give up on commitment, community, and compassion.

First, when we become self-reliant, we tend to give up on our daily commitments to Jesus, meaning that we don't read the Bible or pray. We decide that we already know the scriptures, and talking to God can't do anything for us. We don't have time for that. So, we think less about God and give up on commitment. 1 Timothy 3:16-17 tells us that "[16] All Scripture is breathed out by God and profitable for teaching, for reproof, for correction, and for training in righteousness, [17] that the man of God may be complete, equipped for every good work." If we want to become mature in the faith, knowing how to help those struggling or sinning, we must commit to spending time in the Word daily. It's the only way we can become righteous and ready for the good work God assigns us.

Second, we give up on our Christian community. We assume we no longer need our Christian brothers and sisters and will be fine with those in our immediate earthly family for company. We think we can grow in faith on our own, choosing to watch services online rather than engaging in real fellowship. Conveniently enough, we're also giving up the accountability we will face if we fail to live up to God's Word. The Bible warns us about "not neglecting to meet together, as is the habit of some, but encouraging one another, and all the more as you see the Day drawing near" (Hebrews 10:25). We also need our Christian body to lift us with godly encouragement, as we may not find it anywhere else.

Finally, we also give up on compassion. We think less about other people and their needs and focus instead on ourselves. We can't help, serve, or bless anyone because we're focused on our own problems and desires. Scripture tells us, "Finally, all of you, have unity of mind, sympathy, brotherly love, a tender heart, and a humble mind" (1 Peter 3:8). The Bible calls us to have a unified heart of brotherly love and sympathy for one another. We should reach out to others in faith and love when they are hurting. And, just like surrendering, the scriptures do not make this optional.

I believe that if any person, whether they are a follower of Jesus or not, gives up on living a life of commitment, community, and compassion, they aren't living their best life. Still, this is especially true if you're a Christian. If you are a Christ-follower lacking in these areas, I urge you to reevaluate your life and priorities. God has so much more in store for you. Throughout scripture, we see God's people committed to Him, living in a community with other believers, and demonstrating compassion. This was when they were truly satisfied.

I know that I experience great unhappiness and dissatisfaction when I'm holding onto things I should be giving up and letting go of things I should be holding onto. So, I begin to take stock of what I've got on the shelves. Have I stopped reading God's Word?

Am I no longer praying? Have I lost my desire for community? Am I no longer serving others?

The wonderful thing about Jesus' invitation is that it's always there. The door is always open if I'm holding onto what I should give up. I simply have to surrender, knowing God is pleased with that. He offers blessings. So, what does giving up look like for you? Are you taking off the old self and putting on the new one? What is God asking you to let go of? Don't let your holding on hold you back from the life God has for you. Don't let it cause you to miss out on something greater.

What is God asking you to let go of?

Moreover, what does holding on look like for you? Are you clinging to the fundamentals of your faith, including commitment, community, and compassion? If the answer is no, it's not too late. The door to greater is always open.

A DAY IN THE LIFE

If you're a basketball fan, you've probably heard of Giannis Antetokounmpo. He won the NBA's Most Valuable Player Awards in 2019 and 2020. In 2021, he led the Milwaukee Bucks to their first NBA championship in fifty years. He was also named to the NBA's 75th Anniversary Team that same year, securing his standing as one of the league's greatest players of all time.

Antetokounmpo doesn't view basketball as a fun hobby for which he has a natural flair. He doesn't stuff his face with junk food on his living room couch and brag about how he could dominate the guys shooting hoops on television. Nor does Antetokounmpo practice every day and avoid too many French fries simply so he can keep earning the big bucks. For this serious player, basketball is a way of life. Antetokounmpo thinks about how every part of his daily routine will impact his game and makes sacrifices whenever necessary. When eating breakfast, he thinks about nutrients that will make him stronger. When he's hydrating, he's considering how much water he should drink to maintain his energy. When it's bedtime, he's careful not to stay up too late or sleep until lunchtime because he doesn't want to slow down his game.

When Antetokounmpo goes to the gym, he doesn't just put a good sitcom on the treadmill screen and burn a few calories before going home for dinner. Instead, he chooses specific strength training and aerobic exercises to help him throw a basketball and stay nimble on the court. He knows that some of the activities he could enjoy during his time off could get him injured and impact his ability to play basketball. His big and small decisions in daily life center around one question: will this help me to become a better basketball player? Playing basketball is his purpose, his calling, and his vocation. All other desires must be disciplined into submission so that he can reach his premier goal.

Master of Anything

The truth is that becoming the master of anything requires that your life become oriented around whatever it is you're trying to master. Star athletes don't just walk out from their day jobs onto the court and win championships. Everything they do is customized to help them perform at peak levels.

Most of us aren't basketball stars, but we do have a specific purpose and vocation. If you are a follower of Jesus, your calling is to glorify God in everything you do. Our Lord may have given us some freedom to choose a specific calling. You may be a teacher, a firefighter, a musician, or a stay-at-home parent. Still, our specific calling should always be in submission to the general calling. You can think about how to honor God through your day-to-day activities in whatever line of work to which you've committed. How can you engineer in a way that glorifies God? In what ways does your teaching demonstrate His authority and compassion? How can you be a student who is committed to doing what is right? Can you clean the house in a way that brings Him honor?

Like Giannis Antetokounmpo, every decision we make as Christians should center around one question: what will make me the best follower of Jesus I can be? We need to consider what we can do during the precious hours and minutes of the day that will help us master the art of giving up. When we wake up in the morning, how can we surrender ourselves to Jesus? What should our days look like when we go to work or school? How does surrendering impact our meals? What does the art of giving up look like in our marriages, friendships, and communities? How do we give up during times of rest?

In the Morning

Henry Ward Beecher once said, "The first hour of the morning is the rudder of the day."[4] What you do during those precious moments when you first open your eyes will determine your direction for the rest of your waking hours. If you're serious about living a life of surrender to Christ, you'd be wise to spend them well.

Many of us have no problem ignoring the allure of our alarm clocks. We are more than happy to turn them off and pretend they don't exist. Still, there are other things we can surrender to that often get the best of us in those tender morning hours. Do you surrender to your phone, email, or social media account? Are you taken in by your worries, concerns, and feelings of hopelessness? Is your first order of business obsessing about your to-do list and wondering what else you can cram into your schedule?

I find that when I surrender to my phone in the morning, I'm sinking in its quicksand throughout the day. If I surrender to feelings of sleepiness and don't get out of bed until I absolutely must, I'm tired all day long. If I surrender to negative thoughts or emotions, I'm grumpy until dinnertime. Once I've been swept up in an attitude in the AM hours, it's extremely difficult for me to break out of it during the action-packed parts of the day. It follows that if you're seeking to live as a devoted follower of Jesus, surrendering first thing in the morning is critical. As Matthew 16:24 tells us, we must deny ourselves, take up our crosses, and follow Him. Our first act of surrender in the morning should be to Him.

So what exactly does that look like? The Jewish tradition, which influenced the early church, had a ritual of early morning prayers. Devout followers would say they prayed the moment they opened their eyes before their feet hit the floor. They even had a prayer for their first trip to the restroom in the morning. And traditionally, the first prayer upon waking went like this: "I am thankful before You, living and enduring King, for you have mercifully restored my soul within me. Great is Your faithfulness."[5] It's a prayer of thanksgiving but also one of surrender. Essentially, it says, "God, I did not wake up on my own today. I didn't wake up because of my alarm. I woke up because You are in control of my life and have graciously given me another day to live. I surrender to you, and I trust in your faithfulness." It's a prayer of surrender.

If you're seeking to live as a devoted follower of Jesus, surrendering first thing in the morning is critical.

We see this model of morning prayer in the life of Jesus as well. In the gospels, we read that He woke up early in the morning to pray, be near God, and surrender His will to that of the Father. I love King David's prayer in Psalms 143:8, where he says, "Let me hear in the morning of your steadfast love, for in you I trust. Make me know the way I should go, for to you I lift up my soul." Our first thought in the morning should be of God's steadfast love. How different would our lives be if the first thing we did upon waking was to remind ourselves that God loves us instead of checking to see who sent us an email or wondering if the cat needs to go to the vet? Our attitudes throughout the day could reflect the peace of that moment.

The above is a great verse to memorize for morning meditations, but you can choose another one that speaks to your heart. For example, Psalms 59:16 says, "But I will sing of your strength; I will sing aloud of your steadfast love in the morning. For you have been to me a fortress and a refuge in the day of my distress." Lamentations 3:22-23 tell us, "²²The steadfast love of the LORD never ceases; his mercies never come to an end; ²³ they are new every morning; great is your faithfulness." These verses remind us to take refuge in Him no matter our circumstances, and He will sustain us. Whatever scriptures you choose, it's important to start small since it will take practice to make this a habit. I'm still trying to implement it in my own life. The first thing I try to say when I wake up and get out of bed is, "Good morning, Father. Thank you for giving me another day to live." It's as simple as that.

God is faithful to His Word just like it says in Proverbs 3:6 "In all your ways acknowledge him, and he will make straight your paths." Acknowledging God in the morning will make your way straight for the rest of the day. That doesn't mean that you won't have problems or that everything will be sweet and easy. What it does mean, however, is that God will be with you, and He will show you the way forward.

Whatever you surrender to first thing in the morning will most likely continue to govern your thoughts throughout the day. God's principle of stewardship holds true here. If you are responsible with a little, God knows He can trust you with much. And if you surrender through this small act in the morning, you will likely surrender in more significant ways throughout your day and life. 18th-century English pastor George Whitefield once said:

It is often remarked of people in the Old Testament that they rose early in the morning; and particularly of our Lord in the New, that he rose a great while before day to pray. The morning befriends devotion; and, if people cannot use so much self-denial as to rise early to pray, I do not know how they will be able to die at a stake (if called to it) for Jesus Christ.[6]

In the Small Things

If you've ever tried to eat healthily, you know how vital small choices are. Picking whole wheat over white bread isn't a signal to show your friends how body-conscious you are. It's critical to stay in shape. Once you start indulging in a donut here or a Big Mac there, your midsection will begin to betray you. For some folks, it starts a habit of overeating that's difficult to break. Yet discipline can work with the same

If you are responsible with a little, God knows He can trust you with much.

incremental progress. When you choose veggies over dessert or a salad over carbs, you're training your body to crave what's good. You'll start to think of yourself as a healthy person, and it will be easier for you to give up what you'd like to eat now to gain a stronger body later.

Every sacrifice will not be a grand surrender like Abraham surrendered Isaac. In fact, most of our giving up will be composed of small decisions that add up to a life wisely lived. I have to take these mini steps each day. For example, instead of listening to talk radio on the way to work, I can meditate on worship music or take in scripture and instrumental music on the Dwell Bible app. When I'm on the job, and things are slow, I could find a new way to serve my company rather than scrolling through social media or shopping online. Indirectly, I surrender to the Lord because I want to be an exemplary witness of integrity to those in my workplace. The same holds true when I respond in grace when annoyed with someone or refuse to pass along a juicy piece of gossip. I'm making small offerings that demonstrate God is the most important focus of my life. And when it's time to make a big decision, I will have trained my heart to choose what's best.

Not every day is a give-up-your-dream-and-move-to-another-state day. Instead, we choose to listen to our families rather than catch up on the latest celebrity news. Or we decide to read a Christian novel rather than fill our minds with junk. God sees these moments, and He is helping you to master the art of giving up. He knows that, in the end, surrendering is what will make you complete.

SURRENDERING FOR OTHERS

As we saw in the last chapter, there are many ways that we can structure our days to honor the Lord. We can make small decisions to honor Him with the precious minutes and breaths He gives us. Many of these choices are for our own benefit. When we choose to drink only one cup of coffee or listen to worship music rather than something negative, we become more peaceful and stronger. At the same time, we are helping others because our acts of surrender also benefit them.

Jesus the Servant
Many of us find ourselves overwhelmed by days saturated with important things to do. We have children to raise, money to earn, and meals to cook. It's tempting to believe that we don't have

time for service or that we can make it a priority sometime in the future when our schedules are less demanding.

It's important to note that Jesus, the King of the Universe, never saw Himself as above serving others. In fact, He always assumed a giving up, self-denying posture of a servant. The night before He was crucified, Jesus had a final meal with His disciples. At one point, He stood up, took off His outer garments, and wrapped a servant's towel around His waist. Then Jesus filled His basin with water and washed His disciples' feet. While He did so, He began talking to His disciples about what it means to love one another. True love is not a warm feeling and isn't worship of another's talents or attractiveness. Rather, it is an act of self-denial that considers the needs of others ahead of our own.

In John 13:34-35, He told us, "[34] A new commandment I give to you, that you love one another: just as I have loved you, you also are to love one another. [35] By this all people will know that you are my disciples, if you have love for one another." This is a powerful statement from our Savior. People will know that we are His disciples by our love for each other! The way we serve and care about others will identify us to the world as Christians.

Jesus, wrapped in a servant's towel that was still wet and dirty from washing the disciples' feet, continued to teach the disciples. In John 15:13, He told them, "Greater love has no one than this, that someone lay down his life for his friends." Your acts of self-denial aren't only intended to strengthen your relationship with God. They are designed to bless others. You are not simply sacrificing to Him. He has put others in your life for you to serve. Every day, we should ask ourselves whose feet we will wash and for whom we will sacrifice our desires. Whom are we going to lay our lives down for today?

Throughout His teachings from John chapters 13-15, Jesus continued to drive home this message. Just as He denied Himself for us, He calls us to deny ourselves for one another. As He served us, we should be willing to put ourselves second for the well-being of those around us. Serving isn't easy. Giving up what we want doesn't come naturally so someone else can benefit. In the end, however, the blessings are incalculable.

In Parenting

Parenting is one of those tasks in which we often end up sacrificing for others even when we don't plan to. Your time, money, and home are no longer yours alone. You spend your days working, cooking meals, and doing laundry for the benefit of someone helpless to do them without you. Beyond that, the Bible commands that we discipline our children. This means they may often dislike us even while we give up our comfort for their welfare. Still, what about our child's spiritual life? Are we called to deny ourselves for that too?

We often think of Job from the Bible in terms of His steadfast faith in the face of great suffering. He isn't commonly known as an outstanding, sacrificial dad, but he was. Job 1:4-5 (NIV) tells us,

> [4] His sons used to hold feasts in their homes on their birthdays, and they would invite their three sisters to eat and drink with them. [5] When a period of feasting had run its course, Job would make arrangements for them to be purified. Early in the morning, he would sacrifice a burnt offering for each of them, thinking, "Perhaps my children have sinned and cursed God in their hearts." This was Job's regular custom.

Job was such a sacrificial dad that he made sacrifices on his children's behalf. He took their purity and holiness into his own hands. In today's world, raising children with a commitment to holiness is becoming increasingly difficult. There is sin waiting for them in almost all the videos, games, and movies available. We can't simply turn them over to the school or church youth group and hope they will develop righteousness. It must be constantly reinforced in our homes.

Are we praying for our children to become strong, godly, and committed to doing what is right? Do we practice daily devotions and prayer with them? Can we model teaching and serving in the church? What kinds of charitable activities can we get them involved with, even at a young age? How can we talk to them about adhering to God's principles even when everyone else is indulging in sin?

In a world where many parents are content with children who stay out of trouble, we must teach them how to shine in the darkness. The Bible tells us that "You are the light of the world. A city set on a hill cannot be hidden" (Matthew 5:14). We should make all the sacrifices we can to ensure that our children grow up to love the Word of God. There will come a day when we will no longer be in a position of authority over them. Therefore, it's critical to use the years of child-rearing to honor the Father and inspire our children to be holy. God wants to raise priestly parents in this generation who are willing to sacrifice and love their children as Job did.

In Marriage

It may sound like an odd statement, but I believe that God wants us to give up when it comes to our marriages. If you have a spouse, it's time to think about how you're washing their feet or laying down your life for them. Paul tells husbands in Ephesians to lay down their lives the way Christ loved His church and gave Himself up for them (Ephesians 5:25). Similarly, wives are called to submit themselves to their husbands as God's people submit to Him (Ephesians 5:22-23).

What makes this kind of sacrificial relationship easier is coming to terms with the fact that, once you are married, you no longer belong to yourself. In 1 Corinthians 7:4, Paul writes, "For the wife does not have authority over her own body, but the husband does. Likewise, the husband does not have authority over his own body, but the wife does." Husbands no longer belong to themselves but to their wives. Wives are no longer just individuals. They belong to their husbands as well.

Paul calls the sacrificial nature of the marriage relationship a mystery. It would seem to the natural mind that if a husband or wife is always sacrificing for the other, nothing will ever get done. Still, God seems to bless it. For example, a husband may stop going "out with the guys" on the weekends and instead commit to spending most of his time with his wife. She will, in turn, feel cherished and cared for, making the work she does for the family easier and more fulfilling. Similarly, a wife may give up her daily "me-time" to fix meals that her spouse appreciates. He knows she has been thinking of him and feels more deeply respected. This could inspire him to be more of a leader at church and in the workplace.

I always tell couples that the most successful marriages are the ones that are the most sacrificial. In some cases, it helps to have a conversation about what each partner will value. Some ladies, for example, will expect a traditional partner who will "bring home the bacon" and take care of the family's financial needs. Others are looking for someone to support their professional lifestyle by helping with chores and child-raising. Similarly, some husbands feel adored when their

The most successful marriages are the ones that are the most sacrificial.

partners are happy housewives who like to make their home a warm and tidy place for the family. Others are looking for verbal affirmation or physical affection to feel appreciated. Don't assume you know what your partner needs because you are aware of what you want. Make sure you discuss what you can do to make your spouse feel more valued. You shouldn't be afraid to make loving sacrifices, as they will pay off in the end.

In Community

Some folks aren't married and don't yet have a family. That doesn't mean you're off the hook! The art of self-surrender is just as important in our church communities as in our homes. Is there someone in your community who needs a spiritual mother or father? Are there individuals you can make meals for or offer them free babysitting? Is there a widow or widower who would love to have someone take them out for coffee? Does your church need a Sunday School teacher, a guitar player, or a Christmas play set builder?

There are always ways to give of yourself, your resources, and your time to make your church community better. You may believe that you don't have what it takes to truly serve the Christian community, but God has placed you where you are for a reason. In Galatians 6:2, Paul tells us to "Bear one another's burdens, and so fulfill the law of Christ." This seems like a simple commandment. Others have problems that weigh them down, including physical issues, financial losses, and emotional needs. We can bear those burdens by filling in wherever we can.

The early church in Acts took these commandments to heart, selling their possessions and donating to those in need. It transformed their community. Believers and non-believers alike were marveling at the goodness of God. Imagine what it would be like if today's church demonstrated the same kind of selflessness in a world full of greed and hypocrisy.

Beyond that, we need to think of our community as extending beyond the church and into our neighborhoods, schools, and workplaces. Giving up at work means that we learn to submit to authority. If someone is in a position above us, we can withhold unsolicited opinions and focus on the tasks we've been assigned, provided that no one is asking us to contradict God's word. We can learn to be the best students or employees possible and thus reflect our faith in a positive light. This means completing tasks on time with integrity and enthusiasm. In Matthew 5:16, Jesus tells us, "In the same way, let your light shine before others, so that they may see your good works and give glory to your Father who is in Heaven." Your excellent work at school or home could inspire someone else to finally turn to Jesus and give Him glory.

Moreover, if you are the person in authority, you can treat those entrusted to you with patience, kindness, and fairness. Your employees may take a second look at Christ once they realize that you are indeed the person of grace and character they have always wanted to work for. Our expressions of outward surrender in community, work, and school are never just between God and us. Instead, they are demonstrations of sacrifice so that others can know and experience God's love. When we learn to sacrifice the way God does, we learn to love the way He does.

In Rest

During our waking hours, tasks like parenting, marriage, work, and community require us to sacrifice and demonstrate God's love. This can be exhausting! Finally, it's time to go home and rest. It's essential, however, to realize that our times of rest can also be hours of self-surrender. The key here is surrendering to the right things and the right Person. Streaming your favorite shows, playing phone games, or reading a good book can all be restful. Yet Jesus offers rest that other things can't. In Matthew 11:28-30, He tells us,

> [28] Come to me, all who labor and are heavy laden, and I will give you rest. [29] Take my yoke upon you, and learn from me, for I am gentle and lowly in heart, and you will find rest for your souls. [30] For my yoke is easy, and my burden is light.

If we run to Jesus instead of flipping on Disney+, social media, or reality TV shows, we'll find a rest nothing else can provide. Other forms of relaxation aren't necessarily wrong. There's no reason to think you're a terrible Christian if you do anything besides read the Bible and turn out the light before you go to sleep. Still, if Jesus is your primary source of rest, all other forms of repose become more satisfying and enjoyable.

Perhaps resting means gathering with friends and family and just talking about the day as it ends. What did God do for you? How did He lead and guide you? What did you learn about Him throughout the day? Give thanks for answered prayers, as well as for those yet to be answered. The next time you've had a bad day, try not to surrender your difficulties to Netflix or Facebook. Instead, surrender to Jesus. Rather than helping you turn your mind off or suppress your problems, He will be a source of comfort and provision during your time of need.

Finish your day off the way you started. As you close your eyes, offer your mind, heart, and soul to God. Thank Him for sleep and for sustaining you throughout the day. Ask Him to fill you with rest and rejuvenate you through the night for another sunrise if He lets you see it.

The Jewish tradition regarded sleep as a minor death where you entrusted your soul and well-being to God. Even sleeping, then, is an act of surrender. Psalms 4:8 says, "In peace I will both lie down and sleep; for you alone, O Lord, make me dwell in safety." Our vocation as followers of Jesus is to glorify Him in everything we do. We must always consider this as we organize our days, making big and small decisions. What will help me live in a way that glorifies God? How can my day-to-day living help me master the art of giving up? In the end, you will be glad you included Him in all your plans.

THE BRIDE'S SIDE

Chapters Nine and Ten are told from the perspective of Kai's lovely bride, Annette.

I have always loved weddings. Any excited bride knows the preparation is half the fun. Over the years, I've been paid to do things like wedding coordination and hair for the big day, all of which energizes me to the max. I can think of one ceremony on top of a mountain that required a two-hour drive there and back. I didn't mind at all. My favorite weddings are the ones Kai officiates because we get all this extra time together. The wedding day becomes our date night, with Kai looking all handsome and me in a new dress. We get to have dinner and dance the night away. What's not to love?

At one wedding, I remember, the ceremony was about to start, and the groom asked me to write something on a pallet of wood cut into the shape of a heart. He showed me a photo from

Pinterest that read, "Pick a seat, not a side. You're loved by the groom and the bride." I had never seen that in all my years of coordinating weddings. I completed the sign, and as guests began to arrive, I invited them to sit anywhere.

Traditionally, guests walk into a wedding and must choose who they are there to see. Are they friends of the bride or the groom? It creates a bit of tension. Some people don't want one of the spouses-to-be to have a full side while the other suffers a sparse showing. Other guests believe that choosing a side means you care more about one partner than the other. It can result in all kinds of gossip and drama, which is not uncommon at weddings. There may even be some competition between the two sides that starts the day on a cold foot.

Imagine what would happen if someone arrived at the wedding and told the groom, "I really don't like your choice of a bride, but I love you and will support you no matter what." What would the groom say? My husband Kai isn't usually confrontational. Still, if someone had told him something like that, he would have cordially invited them to stay home at our wedding. It isn't that I don't have flaws or want to be best friends with everyone. It's because I'm his choice, and he is proud of me.

We must both be the Bride and love the Bride.

According to the Bible, the Church is the Bride of Christ (Ephesians 5:25-27). We are His choice. We must both be the Bride and love the Bride. We must both be the Church and love the Church. Though Jesus is the Head, we are the body. We must dress our hearts to be ready for the big day.

Throughout this book, Kai has talked about the central focus of "giving up" as a believer in Christ. While I read through it, an important question keeps popping into my head: Do I love Christ's Bride, the Church, the way He does? I know Jesus wants me to, but I'm often unsure how to get there. How do I show up to the wedding ready to love both the Bride and the Groom?

The Bride's Three Cs

In Chapter Six, Kai talked about the three things we often "give up" that we should hold onto. They are commitment, community, and compassion. Unfortunately, we are prone to give up our commitment to Christ and become self-reliant instead. If we give up here, we're not going to hear His heart for how He loves the Church.

Some people give up on the community of faith, figuring they don't need the Church to help them grow in love or faithfulness. Or we criticize the Church, speaking ill of the Bride. There will always be a movement of people who are okay with Jesus but want nothing to do with the community of believers. These "lone ranger" Christians may think they are avoiding hurt, but they will eventually find a solo Christian walk to be an uphill climb. Sometimes, we think we know everything and proudly approach the Church. We demand that it serve us rather than the other way around. We've all heard jokes about people leaving churches because the church café stopped serving their favorite coffee. Yet some people do approach the body of Christ as consumers. This is not the model Jesus set out for us.

Finally, some church members ultimately give up on compassion. They think less about the body of Christ and more about themselves. Their primary focus is on their own families and well-being. I fully believe in healthy boundaries, but we live in a more insular age than ever. Technology and the pandemic quarantine have made it easy for us to isolate and avoid much contact with those outside of our immediate families. "Staying away" has become a virtue. We forget that we are not islands, but humans made to live and work together.

Sometimes, there are valid reasons to keep our distance. Still, it's so vital that we keep our motives before the Lord. We need to care for our bodies, but we should be tending to our souls simultaneously. The kind of rest that self-care provides should never be a substitute for Sabbath rest. Staying in on a Sunday or keeping your evenings to yourself will give only empty repose because it's not what Jesus leads us to do. In all my years in ministry, I've had many people answer with an adamant "No!" when I asked them to love and serve the Church. The problem is they still haven't asked Jesus for His opinion. He said it was better to give than to receive (Acts 20:35), so it is essential we don't give up in the areas designed to satisfy and bless our lives.

If your first response, when asked to make a sacrifice, is to protect your time, you may need to rethink your priorities. You could be worried about your sleep, resources, or weekends, but Jesus put His Bride first. He was generous and laid down His life. Instead of protecting Himself, He entered an unyielding covenant that allowed us to become covenant people.

We Are a Covenant People, Not a Contractual People

We must understand that our relationship with Jesus is a covenant, not a contract. This is a vast theological concept to unpack, but I want to focus on how it impacts our relationships with other Christians. Contractual relationships are based on two parties fulfilling two different sets of obligations. If one of the parties doesn't meet their obligation, it violates the contract. I could make a long list of reasons this wouldn't work in the Church. We all fall short and let one another down. In addition, everyone has their unique personality, values, and priorities that sometimes clash with those of others.

In a covenantal relationship, however, you sacrifice yourself for the needs of another. This is the type of relationship Jesus created when He died for us on the cross. We owe it to one another to keep loving even when we feel like this type of giving up is too much. After all, Jesus paid the highest price, His own life, for the sake of those who didn't deserve it.

Keeping a covenant means we will continue to serve our brothers and sisters even when they can't repay us the way we want. We need to keep serving them even when they annoy us or when we have strong disagreements. Moreover, remaining in a covenant means there will be a cost to us. God calls us to embrace it.

Embrace the Cost

As many of you know, replacing a home air conditioning unit can be quite pricey. Usually, I would be wrecked by the news that I had to make this type of investment. However, when an inspector told us that our current unit was too small, I decided to embrace the future reality. We always knew we would need a new air conditioning unit one day. The quicker we accepted that, the better off we would be. Five months later, we had our unit replaced even though it came with a hefty price. The temperature is now quite comfortable in our home even when outside conditions are suffocating.

If you're a parent, you know what it's like to make sacrifices during those years when your kiddos won't sit still. I used to watch my son Theo's every move, making sure he didn't dart across the street, take candy from a stranger, or try to eat something attractive yet inedible from the lawn. During that time, if I had taken Theo somewhere and expected to have a deep, uninterrupted conversation, I would

When we sacrifice for the Church, we must expect it will cost us something.

have felt tired and irritated. However, once Kai and I embraced the reality that we were parents of a toddler with boundless energy, we knew what to expect. And we relished the moments of joy that peaked through the clouds everywhere we went.

When we sacrifice for the Church, we must expect it will cost us something. Loving and serving one another is never free. Fortunately, Jesus went ahead of us to show us the pattern. The apostle John was a great storyteller. He knew that to understand the gravity of love, we must first understand the nature of betrayal. John invited us to see the selfish heart of Judas as it contrasted with the love and selflessness of Jesus. It's important to understand that not every "no" in answer to a request for church service equates to a betrayal. Still, we must be aware of our tendency to put ourselves first. Our human nature governs our approach to the Church, and our natures have been soiled with things like hurt and trauma. That's why Jesus is there amid all of it. Look at what happened in John 13:1-5, 12-17, and 34:

> [1] Now before the Feast of the Passover, when Jesus knew that his hour had come to depart out of this world to the Father, having loved his own who were in the world, he loved them to the end. [2] During supper, when the devil had already put it into the heart of Judas Iscariot, Simon's son, to betray him, [3] Jesus, knowing that the Father had given all things into his hands, and that he had come from God and was going back to God, [4] rose from supper. He laid aside his outer garments, and taking a towel, tied it around his waist. [5] Then he poured water into a basin and began to wash the disciples' feet and to wipe them with the towel that was wrapped around him.

> [12] When he had washed their feet and put on his outer garments and resumed his place, he said to them, "Do you understand what I have done to you? [13] You call me Teacher and Lord, and you are right, for so I am. [14] If I then, your Lord and Teacher, have washed your feet, you also ought to wash one another's feet. [15] For I have given you an example, that you also should do just as I have done to you. [16] Truly, truly, I say to you, a servant is not greater than his master, nor is a messenger greater than the one who sent him. [17] If you know these things, blessed are you if you do them."

> "[34] A new commandment I give to you, that you love one another: just as I have loved you, you also are to love one another.

Jesus was quite clear that we should emulate how He gives in two crucial ways: truth and right identity. In terms of truth, we see Jesus acknowledge in verse three that God had given everything into His hands. Similarly, we can acknowledge this by accepting that our gifts, talents, and resources originate with the Father. We can lay it all back down at His feet. In terms of identity, Jesus knew He was returning to the Father one day. It strengthened Him to serve first and later sacrifice His life. He tells us to do the same because no servant is greater than His master (John 15:20).

Ephesians 5:1-2 tells us, "[1] Therefore be imitators of God, as beloved children. [2] And walk in love, as Christ loved us and gave himself up for us, a fragrant offering and sacrifice to God." Jesus gave himself up for us, and we are to imitate Him. Doesn't that sound like the Jesus we saw in John 13 who was willing to wash His disciples' feet?

The Bride and Groom

Later in this chapter, Paul tells us how the harmony between Christ and His Church is like harmony between a bride and groom. A husband must love his wife as Christ loves the Church, and a wife must submit to her husband as the Church submits to Christ. In Paul's letter to the Church in Ephesus, He is writing in the context of community:

[22] Wives, submit to your own husbands, as to the Lord. [23] For the husband is the head of the wife even as Christ is the head of the Church, his body, and is himself its Savior. [24] Now as the Church submits to Christ, so also wives should submit in everything to their husbands.

[25] Husbands, love your wives, as Christ loved the Church and gave himself up for her, [26] that he might sanctify her, having cleansed her by the washing of water with the word, [27] so that he might present the Church to himself in splendor, without spot or wrinkle or any such thing, that she might be holy and without blemish. [28] In the same way husbands should love their wives as their own bodies. He who loves his wife loves

himself. [29] For no one ever hated his own flesh, but nourishes and cherishes it, just as Christ does the Church, [30] because we are members of his body. [31] "Therefore a man shall leave his father and mother and hold fast to his wife, and the two shall become one flesh." [32] This mystery is profound, and I am saying that it refers to Christ and the Church.

What a mystery indeed! Christ washes the Church so that we stand in splendor before Him. I just can't get away from all the bridal stories that so beautifully illustrate this idea. At one wedding, I was helping a bride and realized that the outer layer of her dress, made from tulle, was incredibly wrinkled. One of her sweet friends jumped in and frantically steamed the whole thing until it was pristine. She was thrilled to see her friend happy and never complained.

In a wedding party, there are always two different kinds of people. The first are those who grudgingly accept the invitation to share the day. They complain about everything once they do. They hated the dress; the tux was too expensive; the travel was inconvenient. They are usually selfish and expect the bride and groom to cater to them. They are accommodating the couple, so they expect them to try to make them comfortable.

On the other hand, some are just excited to help! They stay late, serve your family, and bring you water and food when you start to shake. They don't criticize your tears or nerves and walk down the aisle with grace and poise.

Which one are you? Are you the one who serves and loves so the Bride is without a spot or wrinkle? This is the Bride Jesus longs for. I know I always want to be the one who sacrifices so the Bride of Christ will flourish and grow into something beautiful.

THEY WILL KNOW US BY OUR LOVE

When a bride is loved well, she spends her life thriving. She knows she is adored unconditionally so that she can cultivate the best parts of herself, including her gifts and interests, without worry. You won't find her complaining or trying to prove herself. Instead, there is a confident grace as she engages in pursuits in which God has called her to succeed. She learns to live as a loved creature whose beauty of character will matter for all eternity.

In the same way, the church that builds itself up in love flourishes and grows. The imagery in Ephesians 4:16 is lovely when it tells us, "from whom the whole body, joined and held together by every joint with which it is equipped, when each part is working properly, makes the body grow so that it builds itself up in love." As in a healthy marriage, each member has an important role. If they are faithful, the result is a masterpiece of love and maturity, which the world cannot help but notice.

Built-Up in Love

To understand what it means to build one another up in love, we've got to move forward in the text. Look at what is says in Ephesians 4:20-25:

> [20] But that is not the way you learned Christ!— [21] assuming that you have heard about him and were taught in him, as the truth is in Jesus, [22] to put off your old self, which belongs to your former manner of life and is corrupt through deceitful desires, [23] and to be renewed in the spirit of your minds, [24] and to put on the new self, created after the likeness of God in true righteousness and holiness. [25] Therefore, having put away falsehood, let each one of you speak the truth with his neighbor, for we are members one of another.

This passage talks about how we bridle ourselves for the body of Christ. We must put off our old selves and learn to control the desires of our sinful nature. Lust, greed, and malice will wreak havoc on the church body. In addition, we should commit to the righteousness of Christ, which involves putting away falsehood. Unfortunately, sometimes relationships, non-Christian and Christian alike, are often shot through with dishonesty. People will say flattering things to someone and then make them sound like a slob behind their back. We must be above that, speaking the truth in love whenever necessary and never resorting to slander. Later in the chapter, we read,

When a bride is loved well, she spends her life thriving.

> [29] Let no corrupting talk come out of your mouths, but only such as is good for building up, as fits the occasion, that it may give grace to those who hear. [30] And do not grieve the Holy Spirit of God, by whom you were sealed for the day

of redemption. [31] Let all bitterness and wrath and anger and clamor and slander be put away from you, along with all malice. [32] Be kind to one another, tenderhearted, forgiving one another, as God in Christ forgave you (Ephesians 4:29-32).

This passage deals first-hand with how we treat the Bride. We must let go of our grievances toward those in the church body, refusing to harbor grudges. Moreover, we must treat one another with kindness, tenderheartedness, and forgiveness. What bride wouldn't want a husband who let go of offenses immediately and always treated them tenderly? We need to be sensitive to the needs of others, even when they hurt us. Do you need to take someone in your community who needs an understanding ear out for a coffee? Your empathy could be the voice of compassion they thought they would never hear.

The world will recognize a Church whose love is holy and attractive. Jesus says that they will know we're His disciples by our love. In some ways, the Covid quarantine brought out the worst in many Christians. We saw a year of political and cultural divisions and moral failures. Beyond that, the enemy of our souls continues to accuse the Bride. He will accuse until God silences him at the end of time. I don't care about what the enemy says. I am, however, concerned about what we say about ourselves.

Imagine a wedding day when the bride continually criticizes herself, says she feels ugly, and hates her vows. It would cause tremendous confusion. If she continues this attitude, she will wonder if the groom is suitable for her and if he even loves her. Yet we wonder why there are so many "runaway brides" in our churches. If we aren't treating others with love and care, they will eventually leave, looking for worth and value in people, places, and things that can't satisfy their deepest longings. But it matters so much more when the world sees God's people love the church and lay their lives down for her.

In John 13:34-35, Jesus said, "[34] A new commandment I give to you, that you love one another: just as I have loved you, you also are to love one another. [35] By this all people will know that you are my disciples, if you have love for one another." If we are to live out our mission, we can't omit Jesus' command to love one another as He loves us. He gave up His life for the Bride. If we want the world to see the goodness of the Bridegroom, we must always follow this command. Then, we can invite others into healthy, thriving, love-filled communities with plenty of serving, giving up, and loving the church.

Three Ways to Love

When we look at the early church, we see individuals loving one another, selling their possessions for each other, and serving without question. As a result, God added to them daily those who were being saved (Acts 2:42-47). To be entrusted with that blessing, we must begin by loving the Bride. How can we practically do that?

Thankfully, the scriptures are replete with practical advice for showing love to one another. In fact, we can find stockpiles of wisdom just by looking at the second verse of the scripture passage we read earlier: "Be kind to one another, tenderhearted, forgiving one another, as God in Christ forgave you" (Ephesians 4:32). Presented here are three critical ways to love from which we can learn so much.

First, we must be kind. Kindness was a fruit of the spirit before it was a buzzword or a bumper sticker. A member of our church family once told me she visited her son at his church. She was very taken aback by how welcoming everyone was. It was a small body of believers, but she was sure that every single person there had greeted her. Can you imagine being greeted every Sunday by everyone in your church? This church member said she felt very loved and important, but it made her examine her attitude toward newcomers. Now she finds herself asking,

"Did I greet everyone?" each week. Greeting those who visit your church is no small thing. Romans 16:3-16 is a wonderful example of this. It's thirteen verses on how to greet others! It's the doorway by which we show love to those who step into our buildings. N.T. Wright put it this way when discussing Ephesians 4:25-5:2:

> Kindness is a virtue not often considered, but it remains central to what Christianity is all about. The reason for this is stated clearly at the end of this passage: kindness is one of the purest forms of the imitation of God. How would it be if God always made snide or bitter remarks at us? What would worship and prayer be like if we thought God had been talking about us behind our backs, putting us down to others? How would we feel if we couldn't trust God to tell us the truth if he constantly lost His temper with us? Well, what do people think if that's what we're like? Wouldn't it be better in every way to be like God?[7]

The author made an important point. What kind of God are we showing people if we make nasty remarks about them or talk unfairly about them behind their backs? Would they quickly come to trust Him with all their hearts? Or would they turn away, feeling God isn't a safe refuge? How we treat one another is critical to the long-term health of our churches and our souls.

Secondly, we should be tenderhearted. If you are married or have any close relationships, you know that tenderness can change the nature of a difficult conversation. Corrections are sometimes appropriate, but a tender tone will help the medicine go down. Your community members may lean a little closer when you soften your approach. No one will want to be near you if you're too prickly. Engaging in gentle, meaningful conversations and checking in on those who need you is essential. Love is a slow process. We should approach others, wondering how we can encourage them. In our small groups, we can find out who needs to feel valued in the Kingdom of God. As parents, we can let our kids know they are brilliant just because of who they are. People will grow and flourish if you show them how enthusiastically Jesus cares for their souls.

Those within the Church must speak well of her. Can you imagine attending a wedding where all anyone does is gossip, criticize, and slander the Bride? This hardly honors the occasion. Remember, the world is watching. You may have heard the expression, "Salute the rank and not the man." Some of us may have difficulty speaking well of those in the Church due to individuals who have caused us harm. If nothing else, show respect because they are still a part of Christ's Bride. While you may need to work through your feelings in private or with a counselor, it's important to represent her well to those outside of the church body.

Those within the Church must speak well of her.

You may remember an episode of *The Office* where Michael Scott tried to give a wedding reception toast for Phyllis, who was the bride as well as his coworker. His speech was chock full of awkward moments, but things ground to a halt once Michael made negative comments about Phyllis' appearance and her high school reputation. The groom, Bob Vance, kicked Michael out for embarrassing and shaming his bride. He stood up and said, "All right, you're outta here!" It was a cringy and hilarious television moment. In real life, however, I don't want Jesus to ever kick me out for not honoring and loving His Bride, for whom He gave His life.

We need to realize that, as a Bride, we married up. Our Groom is perfect. He is altogether lovely and will always exceed our hopes and dreams. When tempted to criticize His Bride, we should stop and magnify our Savior. This will give us the perspective change we need to have a right-heart attitude. How our Savior loves His Church!

Finally, we can love the Bride through our willingness to forgive. Sometimes, offenses are painful. If we give them time to smolder, offenses will grow into a challenging fire. You may suffer from a genuine hurt that simply needs to be brought to light. As difficult as it may be, it's important to bring these wounds to church leaders or Christian counselors who can help you process them properly. God will redeem that hurt if you bring it to Him. When we forgive, we look like Jesus, who always generously forgives. A church that keeps short accounts will be a sweet fragrance to the world.

Walking in Love

You may remember that Ephesians 4:22 told us "to put off your old self, which belongs to your former manner of life and is corrupt through deceitful desires." Without putting off our old ways, we can never arrive at Ephesians 5:1, in which God calls us to be imitators of Christ who love and give of ourselves. Serving is a call we bear no matter what our personality type is. Your church may have a favorite spiritual gifts test that determines the strengths of its members. Some may be great at hospitality, while others are strong preachers. Still, that doesn't excuse anyone from showing love to those who need it. Everyone can be a people person. The way you show it is between you and the Holy Spirit.

I'm always asking trusted friends and the Holy Spirit to show me areas where I'm not loving the Bride. I've asked them to illuminate where I've been easily offended, exasperated, or irritated. I need to replace all of this with love and surrender to the Church, His Bride. When we are walking in love, we will see all kinds of fruit that's ripe for the harvest.

First, we will reap invitation, not isolation. Individuals who accept Christ are not people who hide out as orphans. The Bridegroom has called us to be His Bride, and we should welcome the time spent with other believers. Secondly, we will see forgiveness rather than frustration. Jesus can set us free from lingering hurt and silent division. He will bring peace where there was angst and frustration. Those sick and disappointed by the Church will be restored to the family of God. Finally, we will see faithful sons and daughters rather than fainthearted slaves. We will discover longevity and legacy in the cornerstone of Jesus and fewer children misidentifying themselves as orphans in God's house. There will be more heroes of the faith, like those in Hebrews 11, and fewer prodigal sons.

Your burnout, exhaustion, and hurt may be real, but it doesn't have to take you out. When the body builds itself up in love, we'll be able to walk each other through the burnout and into a place of healing and healthy serving that comes from wholeness. It all stems from loving the Church the way Jesus did.

You're not alone if you've ever been exasperated, disillusioned, or critical of the Church. The Holy Spirit wants to hover over you, bringing healing and restoration. Greater health can come to you and your church body, but we must practice the art of giving up so the Bride can flourish. If you don't yet have a seat at the table, Jesus has made a way for you to be in right relationship with Him. This is a profound mystery but still an invitation. It doesn't have to be complicated. When you believe in your heart and confess with your mouth that Jesus is Lord, you are rescued from a life apart from God. Don't spend any more time lingering outside the open door.

RESCUE MISSION

One Sunday, I supplied the members of my church with little white flags to keep as symbols of their surrender to God. In retrospect, however, the symbol was infinitesimal compared to how grand the act of giving up for God truly is. I am almost embarrassed by those little white flags now because the art of surrender is so momentous. When it is sincere, giving up is an all-encompassing endeavor. Our flags should cover us from head to toe. They should be wrapped around our families and blanketing our houses. Our flags should be so wide that no one who sees us can miss them. Grateful surrender to King Jesus should define the lives of Christians.

A mini flag would only have enough fabric to cover some areas of our lives. For example, we surrender our Sunday mornings or evening devotional time to Him. A larger flag would symbolize giving our entire lives over for the glory of God and the good of those around us. We can do it with Jesus' example and help from the Holy Spirit. The flag is a symbol not only of our surrender to God but of our recruitment to the cause of Christ. We also display our purpose when we wave our white flag of giving up. Our surrender has a consequential mission behind it. When we follow through and live a life of service and sacrifice as Jesus did, we align ourselves with the same purpose and mission He came to Earth to fulfill.

Grateful surrender to King Jesus should define the lives of Christians.

Through Christ's sacrifice and complete surrender of self, He was able to rescue the world. When we live as He did, we also play a part in seeing it saved. Mastering the art of giving up means helping Jesus continue His mission of saving the lost. Therefore, I'd like to devote the final chapters of this book to exploring His rescue mission.

Love Less

I want to invite you to look at Luke Chapter 14. If you're like me, some passages in the Bible may rub you the wrong way, and this could be one of them. You may even wonder if you can do what Jesus asks of us here. I implore you not to shut down or dismiss those thoughts if you find them running through your mind. Instead, begin to wrestle with them and with the words of Jesus. That's exactly how He would like us to read this chapter. He doesn't want us to follow His words blindly. Instead, He hopes we will truly count the cost of what it means to be His follower.

The apostle Paul tells us, "Do your best to present yourself to God as one approved, a worker who has no need to be ashamed, rightly handling the word of truth" (2 Timothy 2:15). We need to study scripture passages with the gravity they were written, ensuring we know exactly what we're getting into. Those given God's Word will be held accountable for how they understood it and put it into practice. Becoming a disciple of Jesus means that we will partner with Him in His mission to rescue the world, build His kingdom, and defeat the powers of darkness. We will be lousy partners if we haven't counted and even embraced the costs. We need to wrestle well. Eternal impact and outcomes are at stake.

During the passage in Luke 14, Jesus was on his way to Jerusalem. He was going there to die on the cross to rescue all of humanity. It was His final act of surrender and the last phase of His rescue mission. Everyone else, however, believed that He was going to Jerusalem to rise in power, overthrow Roman colonizers, and take His rightful place as the King of the World. Even His disciples believed that glorious conquest would be the culmination of His ministry. Jesus used His final moments before great adoring crowds to clarify what was involved in following Him.

> [25] Now great crowds accompanied him, and he turned and said to them, [26] "If anyone comes to me and does not hate his own father and mother and wife and children and brothers and sisters, yes, and even his own life, he cannot be my disciple. [27] Whoever does not bear his own cross and come after me cannot be my disciple." Luke 14:25-27

Jesus presented us with some heavy words here! What do we do with statements such as ". . . hate your own father and mother" and "Hate your own life?" Does Jesus really want us to hate those things? To understand this more comprehensively, we must remember that the New Testament was written in Greek and Aramaic. The English words we translate these passages into are the best representations of the original language we have. Still, the original phrasing contains some subtleties that English can't always convey. The Greek word for "hate" is one of those instances. The term *miseō* (mis-eh'-o) can mean the strong word we often understand hate to be. It's used in other parts of the New Testament to refer to loathing or total dislike for something.

In this passage, however, it simply means to love less. This clarifies some things because we know that the statement seems to contradict some of Jesus' other teachings. We know He wants us to love our neighbors as ourselves (Mark 12:31) and love our spouses as Christ loves the Church (Ephesians 5:25). Jesus doesn't want us to stop loving these people. He simply states we should love them less than we love Him.

Another example of this occurred in Romans 9:13, where the Apostle Paul quoted from Malachi "As it is written, 'Jacob I loved, but Esau I hated.'" It is in reference to God's choosing to bestow covenant promises on Jacob rather than Esau. God chose to grant preferential treatment to Jacob, so His love for Esau was hate in comparison.

We can also look at the parallel of the Luke passage in Matthew 10:37, which states, "Whoever loves father or mother more than me is not worthy of me, and whoever loves son or daughter more than me is not worthy of me." Again, the meaning here is not that we should hate our relatives. It simply means that our love for them pales compared to our adoration for our Savior. I don't know about you, but I love my family a whole lot. Loving Jesus more than them is difficult. It's easier, of course, when my kiddos are acting like wild heathens. Still, in general, it's quite a challenge to love Jesus more than I love anyone or anything.

Jesus says that to be His disciple, we must love Him more than we love anyone or anything else.

Jesus took all this a step further in Luke 14:33, where He stated, "So therefore, any one of you who does not renounce all that he has cannot be my disciple." The Greek word for renounce in this passage is *apotasso*[8], which means "to renounce, forsake." In other words, *to give up.* That's what we've been learning throughout this book: the art of *apotasso.* It can also mean "to take leave of, bid farewell to." If Jesus asked you to say farewell to your family and follow Him somewhere, would you be able to do it? Would you love Him more if He asked you to give up your job? We need to wrestle with this command. Jesus says that to be His disciple, we must love Him more than we love anyone or anything else. We must be willing to give up everything we have.

Love God More

Loving our family or possessions less is a tall order. In reality, focusing on loving something less can lead to anxiety and even an increased obsession with it. When you focus on loving God more, however, the things competing for your affection will naturally fade into the background.

How can you cause your heart to be so focused on God that all other loves become second place? First, you need to obey Him. This means that you do the Biblical thing even when no other Christians are around and when no one is looking. God is close to those who earnestly seek to do His will, however imperfect their journey may be. Secondly, prayer should become a central part of our lives and a natural response to our daily struggles and triumphs. The Bible tells us, "Is anyone among you suffering? Let him pray. Is anyone cheerful? Let him sing praise" (James 5:13). When we feel particularly sorrowful or elated, our natural response is to want to share these emotions with someone who cares for us. Why not let that individual be the only Person who knows every detail of your day and will love you just as much tomorrow?

Giving to God's ministry is also an excellent way to stir your heart for Him. Jesus told us, "For where your treasure is, there your heart will be also" (Matthew 6:21). Are you tithing to church ministries or supporting missionaries and orphans? Could you spend more time serving those who need you, including the lonely, sick, and hurting? When you demonstrate God's love through physical sacrifice, your emotions will naturally gravitate toward praise for your Savior.

Finally, we must learn to forgive others as Christ forgives us. This can be quite difficult, especially if you are the type of individual who is easily hurt. We must, however, remember how much our sin cost our Savior. When we learn to let go of offenses the way He does, we will find emotional freedom and begin to love Him in a fresh and rewarding way. His purpose for your life will then become a beautiful adventure of love, gratefulness, and giving up.

When It's God

If you're like most Christians, you probably wonder when God is truly summoning you and when you're simply feeling a hunch or a calling meant for someone else. For example, you may suspect God is calling you to sell your home and start a ministry in a foreign country. Or perhaps you feel led to leave your job to head down a new career path. Maybe you sense that God wants you to adopt a child, start a new church ministry, or donate a large portion of your income to a missionary.

The first and most important duty in discerning whether your calling is from God is speaking to Him in prayer. Jeremiah 33:3 tells us, "Call to me, and I will answer you, and will tell you great and hidden things that you have not known." When God is leading you in one direction, you can talk openly with Him about it. He will make those secrets known to you. Tell Him your hopes and fears. The Holy Spirit may let you know through agitation if something isn't from God or through a sense of peace that you are discerning His will.

The sacrifice in consideration must, of course, comply with God's Word. He won't, for example, tell you to leave your spouse for someone else or neglect your responsibility to your children. Instead, His calling will lead you to benefit others, putting yourself second so they can grow and thrive. If you believe God is placing a calling on your heart, the next step is to discuss your plans with spiritually mature individuals. Make sure you choose people who will be honest with you. They will tell you if your plans seem off-base or if they believe there is a need that someone like you could fill. God will often confirm His will by making opportunities readily available. For example, you may confide in a spiritual mentor that you sense God wants you to foster a child. The individual may then let you know about a family who has recently had a positive experience with a Christian foster care agency. Or they could tell you about a youth mentoring program that has just contacted your church. God is in the timing when a mission is truly Heaven-sent.

Furthermore, a calling from God will require you to make good use of your spiritual gifts. For example, you may be blessed with the gift of teaching, mercy, evangelism, or wisdom. Your spiritual gifting is different from your educational background. You may, for instance, be an accountant who feels led to start a church or a lab technician who is called to begin teaching Sunday School. If God provided you with the right talents and knowledge, you wouldn't need a degree to get started. Your calling, however, will always require a humble spirit and willingness to learn and grow. You'll find your true self when you're finally ready to give yourself up.

Lastly and most importantly, God's calling will result in His glory. If He genuinely leads you toward a ministry, the credit will ultimately go to Him. You will watch Him save souls, improve lives, and bring peace. Others will see the results and praise, not your ability, but the

God's calling will result in His glory.

perfect saving grace of a Savior. When you follow the will of God, He will reach others in ways you couldn't have imagined on your own.

THE WHY AND THE WHO (RESCUE MISSION PART II)

2,300 feet. That's how far underground the thirty-three miners from Chile were trapped when the main ramp into the San Jose mine collapsed in August of 2010. Authorities were unable to communicate with them. No sunlight was visible. The workers buoyed themselves in the shelter, subsisting on a carefully rationed spoonful of tuna, half a cookie, and a half-glass of milk every forty-eight hours. Fourteen days later, they were able to send a note tied to a probe to the rescuers working tirelessly to secure their freedom. It read, "We are fine in the shelter, the thirty-three of us."

The rescue workers could then send additional food and water to the miners along with first-aid and lighting. Almost every Chilean government agency, NASA, and a dozen corporations from around the world were on the job day and night. On August 31, drilling began. On September 14, Elizabeth Segovia, the wife of one of the miners, gave birth to a baby girl named Esperanza, which is Spanish for "hope." Three days later, on September 17, the hole reached the miners but had to be widened in a second pass-through. On September 30, the rescue capsule was tested and found comfortable. Hope began to grow. A few days later, on October 5, the rescuers found that they were within 160 meters of the trapped miners, making it likely they could be saved sooner than expected. By October 13, the capsule tunnel had finally reached the miners. Twenty-two hours later, the rescuers brought the thirty-third and final man to safety.

Rescue is an amazing thing. When someone sacrifices their welfare to protect another human, we are always in awe. Throughout this book, we've been talking a lot about surrender. Jesus certainly requires a great deal of giving up from those of us who want to be His disciples. Have you ever stopped to wonder why? Why would He ask us to make Him our highest and greatest love? Why do we need to give up everything for Him? Is it because He is an egotist or a narcissist? Is Jesus insecure, requiring our undying devotion to maintain His sense of self-worth?

Some people do view Jesus as self-aggrandizing in this way, and that's why they don't follow Him. Frankly, if I had this view of Jesus, I wouldn't follow Him either. Let's say a politician wants you to vote for him in the next election. During his campaign, he makes it clear that if he gets into office, you would lose your house, pay higher taxes, and earn a lower wage. There is also a possibility your family and friends could turn on you, making life more difficult. Would you vote for such a candidate? Wouldn't you more likely laugh in his face? Who does this person think he is? Why would anyone try to market themselves this way?

Still, isn't that what Jesus said in passages like Luke 14? Isn't He telling us that if we want to follow Him, we must hate our families, give up everything we have, and get ready to carry our crosses to a horrible death? I can imagine the disciples trying to *shush* Jesus at this point. Teachings like this bring bad publicity. They won't build His brand and will turn people away.

Moreover, we know from the gospels that Jesus did, in fact, lose many followers after making statements like this. They decided the heavy teachings were too much. It's possible they had always viewed Him as a merely political figure and believed the sacrifice wasn't worth it.

What if we could change our perspective, though? What if we view Jesus as the leader of a rescue mission rather than a political figure? I think we can envision Him recruiting a team of brave men and women with whom He will navigate dangerous mountain passes to deliver supplies and care to sick and hurting people. As with those rescuing the Chilean miners, they will need to work tirelessly, trying different methods until they know they can reach the suffering men safely. Still, the important thing is the rescue. The important thing is those children who want to see their father again. The important thing is that people strangled by a disaster find their way out of the cave. We can imagine the leader of such an expedition saying things like, "Before you agree to this, know that the path is treacherous. You won't be able to take much gear or supplies for yourself. A personal pack would weigh you down and jeopardize the mission, so you'll have to leave it behind. The terrain is extremely dangerous, and we might not even make it back. Speaking of which, you'll have to get your affairs in order and say goodbye to your friends and family. Who is with me?"

Since He knew the risks involved, it makes sense that the leader would make such heavy statements and serious requests. He didn't want the team members to be surprised by what was required of them. So, which is He? Is Jesus the politician or the leader of the rescue mission?

Jesus clearly was not here to campaign for office. He was on a rescue mission to save souls that were doomed. Luke 19:10 tells us, "For the Son of Man came to seek and to save the lost." Jesus came here knowing there were people who needed Him to make a sacrifice on their behalf. How did He carry out this mission?

In Mark 10:35, we learn, "For even the Son of Man came not to be served but to serve, and to give his life as a ransom for many." Jesus fulfilled His mission by giving up. He thereby gave us the ultimate example of surrender. Jesus is the only One who has completely mastered the art of giving up. It was through this mastery that He fulfilled His rescue mission.

It doesn't stop there. Jesus did His part by living a perfect life and dying a sacrificial, substitutionary death. He rescued the world once and for all. Jesus supplied us with the medicine to cure all humanity of the disease of sin. Moreover, Jesus is in the business of recruiting mere humans to administer this medicine to anyone who needs it. The mission of the church is the same as that of Jesus. He came to seek and save what was lost. In John 20:21, we read, "Jesus said to them again, 'Peace be with you. As the Father has sent me, even so I am sending you.'" Our mission as His followers is always to seek and save.

Jesus is the only One who has completely mastered the art of giving up.

As Christians, our mission looks different than our Savior's, but only by a little. First, we must continue to rescue those trapped in sin and headed for an eternity of destruction. In Matthew 28:19-20, Jesus told us, "[19] Go therefore and make disciples of all nations, baptizing them in the name of the Father and of the Son and of the Holy Spirit, [20] teaching them to observe all that I have commanded you. And behold, I am with you always, to the end of the age."

Going out into the world requires the same sacrifice and service Jesus modeled for us through His life and death. As we discussed in the last chapter, He told us, "²⁶ If anyone comes to me and does not hate his own father and mother and wife and children and brothers and sisters, yes, and even his own life, he cannot be my disciple. ²⁷ Whoever does not bear his own cross and come after me cannot be my disciple" (Luke 14:26-27).

Jesus is not a politician making unrealistic promises. Rather, He is the leader of a rescue mission who is honest about what to expect as His follower. When we understand the "why" behind His requests, we also understand why our love and devotion to Him need to be greater than they are for anyone or anything else. That's what it takes to rescue the world. Our

We are not following a politician; we are following Jesus the Rescuer.

giving up has a purpose. We are not following a politician; we are following Jesus the Rescuer.

Every time we wave our white flags of surrender to Him, we also declare that we are joining His rescue mission to save the world. We are saying that we are ready to give up, *apotasso*, everything. We must be prepared to serve, sacrifice and lay down our lives for others. Then we will genuinely know the rescuing love of Jesus.

The Who

Knowing why God calls us to sacrifice is critical to the discussion of giving up. Still, there's one more tool I want to give you before you become a master of giving up. It's important to know that Jesus is our rescuer and wants to save the entire world. That, however, is an impossible undertaking for someone who isn't Jesus. I cannot sacrifice on behalf of every single person in the

97

world, and neither can you. Yet I can still serve one, two, three, or four people in His name and serve them well.

If you've been practicing the art of giving up, you know it isn't easy to sacrifice on behalf of Christ. It's demanding, and there is a lot to endure, even just for the sake of those who live in our homes. If you are a parent or spouse, you know what it's like to sacrifice daily, even if you don't feel like doing it. Still, it's important not to start as though you, an individual, are responsible for rescuing the entire world. Narrow your focus. Who are your people? What are their names, and how will your surrender impact them? Are they your family members, neighbors, or co-workers? Putting a face on those that need rescuing will motivate you to keep going and pursue your purpose.

This is precisely what Jesus did to help Him endure the mission of giving up on the cross. Rather than thinking about the sacrifice, He focused on whom He made it for. Hebrews 12:2 tells us that we should be "looking to Jesus, the founder and perfecter of our faith, who for the joy that was set before him endured the cross, despising the shame, and is seated at the right hand of the throne of God."

I don't believe that the joy set before Jesus was a "what." I don't believe He endured the cross merely for His own self-aggrandizing glory. I believe that the joy set before Him was a

Put a person in your purpose.

"who." Knowing whom He was sacrificing for helped Jesus endure giving up everything, even to the point of death on the cross. *We are Jesus' joy.* He endured the pain and shame of the cross for you and me. I believe it was our faces and names He was picturing. That is what gave Him the strength to endure.

When thinking about your surrender, you must remember not just the *why* but the *who*. Put a person in your purpose. Who in your immediate sphere of influence will be impacted when you master the art of giving up? For whom are you waving your white flag of surrender?

As we wrap up this book, I want you to carefully consider the size of your white flag. Has it grown while you've been reading? Does it need to expand more so it covers your entire being? Why are you surrendering? Do you believe in the rescue mission, the reason why Jesus is calling us to be His followers? Moreover, who are the important people in your life on whose behalf Jesus calls you to surrender? Raise and lengthen your flag. Commit to mastering the art of giving up. God will be glorified, and the world will be rescued through our efforts.

EPILOGUE:
A TIME FOR
BLESSING

The more we give up ourselves, the more we gain from God. Only when we live with true surrender and service can we experience genuine satisfaction in every area of our lives. In the first two chapters, we discussed how a life of sacrifice begins with self-denial. Then, in Chapters Three and Four, we unwrapped how important it is to know who is asking us to make the sacrifice. Who is this Jesus, the God who requires us to surrender everything to Him to be His follower? When we explored this question, we realized God is trustworthy and deserving of our self-sacrificing love.

In Chapters Five and Six, we dug deeper into the things we should be giving up versus those we should hold onto. Some things are worth sacrificing for the sake of the Kingdom. Still, there are other things to which we should hold fast since God Himself commands that we honor them. They include practices like self-discipline and guarding our hearts and minds. In Chapters Seven and Eight, we looked at what a day in the life of a surrendering person looks like. To master the art of giving up, we should practice surrendering to the commands of Jesus from the minute we wake up until we rest our heads on the pillow at night. In Chapters Nine and Ten, my wife Annette shared some powerful insights about giving up in the context of community and what it means to love Jesus' Bride, the Church. The body of believers isn't perfect, but we must love Her well to honor our heavenly Father. In Chapters Eleven and Twelve, we discussed how the sacrifices involved in following Jesus are easier to bear once we realize we a part of a divine rescue mission to save souls for eternity.

As we reflect on what we've learned so far, we realize that Jesus wants us to deny ourselves, take up our crosses, and follow Him daily. We realize that mastering the art of giving up is a tremendous undertaking. It touches every aspect of our lives as Christ-followers. Giving up is a moment-by-moment discipline. It takes a great deal of work, but it's also quite rewarding. God gives us the unique privilege of watching Him use our surrender for His glory and for the good of those around us. Moreover, He blesses us at the same time. I'm reminded of Jesus' words to His disciples after they said, "Hey, we've given up everything for you. We've left our jobs and families."

In Mark 10:29-30 we read

[29] Jesus said, "Truly, I say to you, there is no one who has left house or brothers or sisters or mother or father or children or lands, for my sake and for the gospel, [30] who will not receive a hundredfold now in this time, houses and brothers and sisters

and mothers and children and lands, with persecutions, and in the age to come eternal life."

Jesus promised they would receive a hundredfold what they have given up both in this life and in the life to come. He told us there would be incredible blessings when we give up for His sake.

For whom are you waving your white flag? Are there others who can find refuge in the protection of its shadow? I encourage you to surrender to Jesus and never second-guess your decision. God will bless you beyond what you can imagine.

About the Author

I've been married to my best friend and partner in life, Annette Eilert, since 2011. And guess what! She's a co-author of The Art of Giving Up. She has two outstanding chapters about loving the bride of Christ that will for sure encourage you in your walk with Jesus. Annette and I have four beautiful kiddos: Myles, Oliver, Theodore, and Eleanor.

In our free time, my family and I love being outdoors playing with our two dogs, swimming in the pool, or climbing up in the tree house. We're also a musical family and enjoy playing music together or having spontaneous dance parties to our favorite pop songs.

Home for us is in Tucson, AZ, where we pastor a great church called Central City Assembly. I served in the United States Air Force for six years, which brought me to Tucson. After serving in the Air Force I restarted my college education at the University of Arizona. I graduated with a degree in Creative Nonfiction Writing. Shortly after graduating in 2015, I became the pastor of Central City Assembly. It's been such a privilege to shepherd God's people and see them learning and growing in what it means to be faithful followers of Jesus.

Endnotes

1   *Arneomi*, Strong's Concordance G720

2   Cady, Nick. "The Statistical Probability of Jesus Fulfilling the Messianic Prophecies." February 18, 2020. www.nick cady.org. https://nickcady.org/2020/02/18/the-statisti cal-probability-of-jesus-fulfilling-the-messianic-prophe cies/.

3   Merriam-Webster.com Dictionary, s.v. "art form," ac cessed September 21, 2022, https://www.merriam-web ster.com/dictionary/art%20form.

4   Edna Proctor. Life Thoughts: Gathered from the Extem poraneous Discourses of Henry Ward Beecher. (Eden borough, 1858), 59.

5   Sefaria: A Living Library of Torah. Sefaria.org, accessed November 16, 2022. https://www.sefaria.org/ sheets/247853?lang=bi.

6   Whitefield, George. "Abraham's Offering Up His Son Isaac." Accessed November 16, 2022. https://www. sermonindex.net/modules/articles/index.php?view=arti cle&aid=971

7   Wright, N.T. Paul For Everyone: The Prison Letters (The New Testament For Everyone), (Louisville, Kentucky: Westminster John Knox Press, 2004).

8   *Apotassō*, Strong's Greek Lexicon G657